PRO BASKETBALL'S LITTLE MEN

Profiles of nine "short" men show how their talents and determination made up for the inches they lacked and brought them success in a game of giants.

PRO
BASKETBALL
LIBRARY

PRO BASKETBALL'S LITTLE MEN

BY RAY HILL

illustrated with photographs

Random House · New York

PHOTOGRAPH CREDITS: Vernon J. Biever, 14, 89, 135; Camera 5/Ken Regan, 102, 115, 118, 125; Carolina Cougars, 58; Malcolm Emmons, 10, 18, 40, 44, 53, 75, 78, 82; Ronald C. Modra, 2–3; United Press International, 1, 27, 31, 34, 92, 110, 139, 143; University of Southern California, 62; Wide World Photos, endpapers, 5, 23, 49, 54, 67, 70, 85, 97, 100, 107, 122, 132, 147.
Cover: Photo by Malcolm Emmons

Library of Congress Cataloging in Publication Data
Hill, Ray.   Pro basketball's little men. (Pro basketball library   9)
SUMMARY: Traces the success stories of nine shorter-than-usual pro basketball stars who made up in skill for what they lacked in height.
1. Basketball—Biography—Juvenile literature.
[1. Basketball—Biography] I. Title.
GV884.A1H49   1974   796.32′3′0922   [B]   [920]   74-4933
ISBN 0-394-82768-6   ISBN 0-394-92768-0 (lib. bdg.)

Manufactured in the United States of America   1   2   3   4   5   6   7   8   9   0

To
**NICK
CURRAN,**
*a little guy who
helped in a big way*

CONTENTS

INTRODUCTION

On the street, a 6-foot-1 man is above average in height. But on the pro basketball court, he is almost a midget. Modern pro basketball is filled with giants. Seven-foot centers abound, as do 6-foot-9 forwards and 6-foot-4 guards. Yet there is a place for the little man in the sport—a very important place.

During the 1950s Slater Martin, the tiny playmaker of the Minneapolis Lakers and St. Louis Hawks, and Bob Cousy, Boston's all-time great, were pioneer small men in the NBA. More recently, Buffalo's sensational Ernie DiGregorio and the Knicks' sharp-shooting Henry Bibby have made the news. Martin and Cousy have had their stories told. In some future book, perhaps, Ernie D. and Henry will gain the spotlight.

This book has chapters on fine, little all-round players like Gail Goodrich, Mack Calvin, Louie Dampier, Nate Archibald and Freddie Lewis. Also featured are small guys with special talents: Norm Van Lier, Dean Meminger, Billy Keller and Calvin

Murphy. All of them were guards 6-foot-1 or under who played in the National Basketball Association or the newer American Basketball Association. Some were superstars in their respective leagues, some were substitutes. If there is one thing they had in common, it was the hardship they had to endure. Each and every one was told at some time in his life that he was too small to play basketball.

And each and every one proved the exact opposite. They earned the respect of their taller teammates and opponents while giving hope to thousands of short youngsters that they, too, might some day succeed in the big time.

When Dean Meminger signed with the New York Knicks, a reporter asked him if his height would cause him trouble. Every little man gets asked that question. Meminger spoke for all of them when he answered, "It's not how tall you are, it's how tall you play."

Ray Hill

1. CALVIN MURPHY

The fans in the Philadelphia Spectrum must have thought an H-bomb had exploded. But, no, it was only a tiny blockbuster named Calvin Murphy. Little Cal, the backcourt ace of the San Diego Rockets (now the Houston Rockets), was the leading scorer in a game with the 76ers late in 1971, his rookie year. The Philadelphia club did everything except nail his sneakers to the floor—and the way he played that night, even that might not have stopped him.

Murphy really cut loose in the fourth quarter. Skittering around the court like an out-of-control midget racer, he ran the 76ers crazy. He brought the ball down and hit on a 24-foot jump shot. Next, it was a 23-foot jumper. Then he faked and went in a few steps for one from 18 feet, then another from 20 feet. After all this rapid-fire gunning, he brought gasps from the Spectrum crowd on a later play. Murphy fired the ball from 25 feet out. When it bounced off the front of the rim, Calvin zipped toward the basket, snagged the rebound and banked it in as teammates and opponents stood staring. A little later, Murphy drove inside to score with a running hook, one of the most difficult shots in basketball, and San Diego took a 99–91 lead.

The 76ers had had enough. Here was the smallest man in the NBA embarrassing them on their home turf. Something had to be done. After a hastily called time-out, they resorted to a defense that looked suspiciously like a zone (which is illegal under NBA rules). Philly employed three guards—Hal Greer, Wali Jones and Archie Clark—and two forwards. The forwards hung back near the basket while the guards played a full-court press. The idea was to trap the Rocket ballhandler and force a turnover. Unfortunately for Philadelphia, the ballhandler was Calvin Murphy.

No sooner had the San Diego whiz started his dribble, than all three 76er guards were swarming around him. Coaches teach their players to pass the ball off when confronted with a zone trap—it is a fundamental tenet of the game. Murphy ignored the fundamentals in favor of basic schoolyard tactics. He threw some head and hip fakes and dribbled right through the pack of defenders!

Calvin was on his way to the basket when Archie Clark fouled him from behind. Murphy calmly popped in two free throws to lengthen the San Diego lead.

Philadelphia fought to within two points, 103–101,

late in the match. San Diego's defense had gone sloppy and it looked as if the 76ers might just pull it out. But Calvin Murphy came through when he was most needed. He took a pass, evaded his three "shadows" and shot over the outstretched arms of the 76er forwards for a 13-foot jumper. That play crushed Philly's spirit. San Diego won, 111–103.

"When Calvin smokes like that," commented teammate Larry Siegfried, "forget it."

Murphy's superb ballhandling was just as important as his red-hot shooting ability in the Rocket victory. "I have confidence in my dribble," he said after the game. "I know what I can do and what I can't do with the ball. You've got to attack the zone. If you lay back, they're going to trap you." He had been anything but trapped. A trapped man doesn't score 27 points (including nine of ten free throws) to lead all scorers, and contribute four rebounds and a couple of assists to boot.

A writer asked Calvin if he was surprised at having such a fine game against a defensive stalwart like Archie Clark. "No," he answered without a trace of bragging, "I'm never surprised at having a good game. I'm just angry I didn't have a better one. I haven't proven anything yet, except that I can last a season in this league. Some said I wouldn't, but I knew I could play. I still make a lot of mistakes—mostly on defense—but size has nothing to do with it."

Murphy's size, of course, had everything to do with

it. All his life, Calvin had to listen to people harp on his small stature. The criticism really came to a head when, at the San Diego rookie camp weigh-in, it was revealed that Murphy was actually only 5-foot-9 and not the 5-foot-10 his college press releases proclaimed. Cynics around the nation shook their heads; how could anyone that short forge a career among the NBA's giants? Some compared his presence in the league to that of the midget player once sent to bat by baseball owner Bill Veeck as a joke.

The doubting and the wisecracks only served to harden the little man's determination. "They said I was too small to play in high school. I made All-America. Then they said I couldn't play in college. I made All-America three years running. Now they say I can't play in the pros. Well, damn, I know I can."

Calvin has been telling—and showing—people what he could do since he was a youngster back in Norwalk, Connecticut. He grew up in pretty tough surroundings. "You had to fight to prove you could live in the neighborhood," he said.

Curiously, he came from a tall family. His father was 6-foot-4, his mother was a six-footer and he had two brothers both well over six feet. "By the time I reached the ninth grade," he recalled, "I knew I wasn't going to grow. So I stopped worrying. I just tried to do the best I could with what I had."

Murphy was considerably quicker and stronger than many of his bigger high school buddies. What's

Calvin Murphy: "Size has nothing to do with it."

more, he had the daring to try anything. In school he ran dashes (9.9 seconds for 100 yards), broad-jumped (more than 20 feet), triple-jumped (45 feet) and even gave football a shot. He wanted to play basketball most of all. Many of his friends thought he was foolish to even try out for the team. After all, he was just 5-foot-7 in his sophomore year.

Calvin soon had them changing their minds. He could dunk the ball as well as any big man on the team, and he could shoot better than anyone. He was an instant starter on the varsity. Scoring 40 and 50 points a game became commonplace for him. Any doubts his pals still had disappeared when Murphy was named All-State his first year out. Later on, he was a high school All-America and scored 62 points in an all-star match.

He carried a big reputation around Connecticut high school circles, but it didn't spread to the New York City schoolyards, the real testing ground for Eastern cagers. "I remember once I went to a schoolyard in Brooklyn and Connie Hawkins [later a pro star with Phoenix and Los Angeles] was king there. I asked to get in the game and he said, 'Later, kid.' I never got in the game. I kid Connie about that now."

The Boston Celtics' general manager and former coach, Red Auerbach, a fine judge of talent, called Murphy "the greatest high school basketball player I ever saw." Lots of colleges agreed with that assessment. Murphy had 235 scholarship offers in his lap by the time he graduated. All the top-name colleges were interested, yet he chose to attend little-known Niagara University in upstate New York. Why? One major factor was that they could arrange to have him twirl the baton during half time at Buffalo Bills games. An aunt had taught him how to twirl when he was very young. Calvin wasn't afraid of being labeled a sissy. He got so good at it that he won an award at the 1964 World's Fair. He liked the idea of being able to show off at pro football games.

And Niagara liked the idea of Calvin's playing for them. He was, naturally, the smallest guy on the team—not that it mattered. Murphy scored like a demon. He averaged 37 points per game in his first varsity year, as a sophomore. He went on to average 33.1 ppg for his three varsity seasons, and to become the fourth-highest point scorer in the history of big-time college basketball. Villanova coach Jack Kraft said Calvin was "the best shooter I've ever seen—pro, college or high school—in all my years. No ifs, and or buts about it."

There were difficulties, however. Niagara lost more games than it won during Murphy's stay. His very first varsity game was an omen of things to come. Calvin burned the nets for 41 points, but Niagara lost to Long Island University, 84–79. His one-man heroics simply weren't enough. The overall caliber of the team didn't improve until his senior year.

Added to the pressures of losing were the pressures to make good grades (he did—graduating with a B

average) and some racial problems. Niagara had very few black students. The rumor got around that Murphy was dissatisfied and that he might transfer to another school. He was quoted in his second year as saying, "There's no social life on campus for us. It gets a little lonely sometimes. Something like a Wednesday night coffee date—we don't have that. We go to Buffalo—20 miles away—when we want any social life."

He stayed put. Eventually, he met and married a Niagara coed, and he spent what spare time he had working as a troubleshooter for the local police. With most of his own troubles overcome, Murphy seemed to have a bright future after graduation.

Up to this time, Murphy's playing career had been filled with distinction. But in the NBA's 1970 draft he received a distinction he could have done without. Calvin became one of the few college super-scorers in history not to be picked in the first round. You had to tear through the record books to find another consensus All-America so snubbed by the NBA.

It was a good year for tall college guards like the much-publicized Pete Maravich, so no one was in a hurry to grab Calvin. San Diego finally picked him on the second round after more than a dozen other players had been claimed. The whole thing left a bad taste in his mouth: "When I wasn't drafted on the first round, like I was sure I would be, pride got involved. I thought to myself, 'I'm sick of proving

The smallest player on the Niagara varsity, Cal was still their biggest scorer.

myself over and over.' So I was going to go with the Harlem Magicians for sure."

The Magicians were an entertainment team styled after the famous Harlem Globetrotters. Calvin's ball-handling and dribbling would have helped pack in the crowds (and his size would make him a curiosity). The Magicians offered him a sizable contract, and Murphy was prepared to sign out of spite. Then he had a talk with a friend, Willis Reed of the New York Knicks. Reed convinced Calvin that clowning with the Mags was a waste of his talent, that he belonged in the NBA. So Murphy swallowed his pride, declined an ABA offer and signed with the Rockets.

The story behind San Diego's 1970 draft was more complicated than it seemed. The Rockets, who had the first choice in the first round, could have taken Pete Maravich. But they couldn't afford his million-dollar price tag and they worried that his flamboyant personality would conflict with that of Elvin Hayes, the San Diego center. Instead, the club picked Michigan forward Rudy Tomjanovich first. Then the Rockets' young scout Frank Hamblen persuaded his team to draft Calvin. Hamblen had been a player for Syracuse University when Murphy was at Niagara. One night Hamblen had seen Murphy bomb Syracuse with 68 points in one game, and understandably, he never forgot that performance.

Plenty of people waited for Murphy to fall flat on his face during his rookie year. But Calvin wasn't about to give them the satisfaction of watching him fail. In a pre-season game between the Rockets and the Los Angeles Lakers, Laker giant Wilt Chamberlain warned Calvin, "If you want to stay on the court, rookie, stay out of the middle."

It was the old veteran-intimidates-rookie routine. Considering Wilt's size advantage—he was nearly a foot-and-a-half taller and perhaps 100 pounds heavier than Murphy—it should have worked. Calvin, however, refused to be intimidated. Soon after the threat, Calvin was dribbling the ball right down the middle. Chamberlain loomed over him. Murphy threw some fakes. Wilt went one way—out of the play—and Cal went another, straight in for an easy lay-up.

A few teams backed up their threats with muscle. Murphy took his lumps. "When he goes down," said Rocket trainer Barry Wyloge, "I close my eyes and say a prayer."

"I'm always being knocked down," Murphy admitted. "But I just pick myself up and keep going. You get used to it. If you keep asking yourself why, you might begin worrying about it. You can't afford to be afraid."

Murphy was the Rockets' sixth man, or chief substitute, for most of his first year, a role he grudgingly accepted. He averaged 15.8 points a game while displaying other extraordinary talents. His coach, Alex Hannum, called him the "fastest man on the dribble in the NBA." Calvin said, "I need less of an opening to squeeze past a defender, and my dribble is so close to the ground that it's tough to steal the ball." NBA commissioner Walter Kennedy stated, "I've seen all the outstanding players of the last 40 years. Calvin has hands as quick as anyone ever."

Super endurance was another of his advantages. "People don't like to guard me because I'll run all night," he said. "If you're 6-foot-5 and 200 pounds, you're in trouble guarding me, because I'll run you to death. And if you get tired, then you're really in trouble, because then you're my size."

Then there was his unbelievable jumping ability. Over his first three years in the league, he outjumped men 6-foot-7, 6-foot-9 and 6-foot-11. He said, "I can outjump a center if I time it right." Elvin Hayes noted that Murphy's powerful legs helped the guard operate "at the 6-4 level."

Hayes took a special interest in Calvin, nicknaming him "Chickadee," because Elvin said he had the young player under his wing. One of the finest centers in the league, Hayes didn't get close to many guys on his club, especially if they had star potential, but Murphy was an exception. The two got along just great although the team lost most of its games.

"I have nothing to worry about with Elvin," Cal noted, "and I don't think Hayes runs the San Diego Rockets. Reading about him and then meeting him, it's two different people.

"We've been more or less in the same situation," he continued. "Constant pressure, always having to carry a team. It's obvious that teams will be posting

His path to the basket blocked by the Royals' Sam Lacey, Murphy tries to pass the ball off to a Rocket teammate.

me [driving toward the basket against him]. I'll be picked off at times under the basket, let's face it. Well, Elvin's the best shot-blocker in basketball. He'll be there to rescue me. I need him."

Sure, there were times when he had to be "rescued." He had his share of bad defensive games, but not as many as his critics had anticipated.

As Murphy put it, "I have to use what I have—speed and quickness—and I practice constantly on being mismatched." His favorite defensive technique was all-out harassment. "I try to get right into my man, to make him work so hard bringing the ball upcourt that by the time he gets into his offensive area, he is giving up the ball because I've played him so hard. I try to force him to go with the ball when he doesn't want to go, so that he has to give it up. Either that or he'll try to post me.

"This is what we hope will happen a lot of times," he revealed. "While they're trying to set up someone one-on-one against me, their four other men are just standing around. When they try to post me, they're usually disrupting the rhythm of their offense."

The Rockets moved to Houston, Texas, following the 1970–71 season, hoping that Elvin Hayes—who had played for the University of Houston—would attract big crowds. It didn't work out that way. Elvin had wanted to stay in San Diego, and the Houston fans resented his attitude. So the Rockets continued their losing ways before scanty audiences. Coaches and players came and went (Hayes was traded to

Baltimore in 1972), but Murphy continued to spark the club.

He averaged 18.2 points a game in 1971–72, 13 the next year and 20.4 in 1973–74. Sometimes he started; sometimes he didn't. His coaches used him where his talents were best suited. Either way, he saw himself as more than just another player. "I think of myself as the pioneer of the little guy," he stated. "If I didn't make it my first year in the pros, people would be second-guessing and third-guessing all the little men who would try later on. They'd say, 'Well, if Calvin Murphy didn't make it, no little man is going to.' "

Calvin did make it, and he spoke for all the little players when he said, "I don't think of myself as being short. I tend to think of myself as average for a man. It's just unfortunate I have to play against people who aren't average."

Unfortunate, yes—for his opponents.

2. BILLY KELLER

Some veteran players can look back with pride at their first game as a professional. Others, like Billy Keller, would rather forget theirs. His first game with the Indiana Pacers was, to say the least, an embarrassment.

It was the season opener in the fall of 1969. The Pacers were playing at home, and the local fans eagerly awaited Billy's first appearance as a pro. The little rookie sat nervously on the bench during the first quarter. Then early in the second, coach Bob Leonard told him to go in. The crowd cheered loudly as he entered the action. Everyone wanted him to do well. Some of the fans had rooted for Billy when he was a star at Indianapolis Washington High School and had followed his career at Purdue University. Keller's prep and college success as a hometown boy and his small stature made him an instant favorite. He was under enormous pressure to succeed.

Maybe he was too anxious to please the fans.

Whatever the reason, as soon as he got the ball Bill threw up a bad shot from 18 feet out. It missed, and the fans groaned. Soon afterward, he popped another from the same distance. More groans. Next, he tried to hit a teammate with a pass that was so wild it wasn't even close. To top it off, the man he was supposed to guard scooted past him twice for scores. Coach Leonard pulled him out of the game. Bill trotted back to the bench with his head high, but his heart was dragging. He got polite applause from the sympathetic onlookers.

He played a bit of the third quarter—more bad shots, more clumsy defense, more sympathetic applause. Luckily, Indiana won the game. If it hadn't, Keller might have taken his poor showing even harder than he did. As it was, he sat slumped before his locker after the match, every mistake he had made flashing through his mind.

A sportswriter friend asked him if he was okay. "Yeah, I guess," Billy responded in a low voice. "You see that bag?" he asked, pointing to his equipment case. "Well, I feel like I've got one foot in that bag and the other in the parking lot. I was terrible. I may not be around here very long."

"Bill," his friend said, "there are 83 games left, and if you're going to be around you have to be the real Bill Keller, not somebody counting mistakes and worrying. I mean, why don't you quit counting mistakes and start thinking what you can do?"

Keller brightened. "You know something? That's

right." He began to smile. "I can't worry myself into a job, can I?"

He had plenty to worry about. Sure, Bill knew there were folks in his corner. But he also knew there were many people questioning his ability. Skeptics, including some pro scouts, gave him little chance to excel in the big time. Keller was only 5-foot-10. Was he capable of defensing a taller man? Was his shooting up to professional caliber? The home opener seemed to indicate the doubts were warranted.

He was, however, just a rookie, and all rookies made errors. What the skeptics didn't reckon with was Billy's greatest strength—his capacity to learn. He learned from talking to people, men like his sportswriter friend, and by watching others.

Back in 1963, Keller earned pocket money by working as an usher at the state high school basketball tournament held in March. The team that won the title, Muncie Central, was led by an undersized backcourtman named Rick Jones. He dominated the action with his uncanny moves. "I was impressed with his quickness and speed," recalled Billy. "So I decided to pattern my play after Jones since he was so successful. When you're small, you have to make up for it—so you do it with speed."

Two years later, in 1965, Billy took Washington High to the championship in the state tournament. He was a good shooter, a fine ballhandler, and few boys could keep up with him when he turned the speed on. He was designated "Mr. Basketball," the highest honor given to a high school player in the state.

Then Keller went to Purdue, and again he had a lot to learn. He had to accept the fact that he was not to be the basketball team's star. When Keller was a junior, sophomore All-America Rick Mount was Purdue's attention-getter. Everyone else, including Billy, took a back seat.

In his 75 varsity games at Purdue, Keller scored over 1,000 points and averaged 14 points a game. Not bad, considering his main duty his last two years was as playmaker—putting the ball in Rick Mount's hands. Thanks to their smooth backcourt, the Boilermakers grabbed a runner-up spot in the NCAA tournament in Billy's senior year (1969).

Billy was drafted by the Pacers on the seventh round, a sure indication that many doubted his ability. He would have to scratch and claw just to get a seat on the bench; no one was going to hand him a job, that was for certain. He knew he was bucking the odds as he drove his 1963 Chevy to rookie camp.

He really stood out among the dozen or so hopefuls. He was, naturally, the shortest player in camp, and his 180 pounds gave him a stocky, squarish appearance uncommon in a guard—his high school teammates had called him "Fireplug." Billy stood out as a player, too. Gradually the others were cut. Keller won a place on the club's ten-man roster.

In the years to come he would prove his value to Indiana over and over again. As a starter and as

Playing for Purdue, Keller fakes a big North Carolina defender off his feet.

sixth man, he would be one of the most important players on a team that would win three ABA crowns in four years.

If anyone had suggested such a thing after Billy's first game, he would have been laughed out of the locker room. Keller tried to take his friend's advice not to let the errors get him down, but he still worried. "Last season I worried about every game," Billy said in 1970. "I wanted to do so well in front of our fans that I really pressed the first couple of months. If I didn't get in a game, I was hurt and I thought, 'Maybe Slick [coach Leonard] doesn't think I can play this guy.' Sometimes I told myself I wasn't getting a fair shot because of my size. I was actually talking to myself a few times. But Slick gradually broke me in on the road. Then he let me play a lot at home and my confidence started to build because I played pretty well at home and people responded."

Rookie Keller took his share of abuse, both physical and verbal. Veteran guards did everything they could to rattle him. "Larry Jones [of the Floridians] used to say things to me, and he'd shove and push to test me. Don Freeman [then with Texas] used to ride me. Louie Dampier [of Kentucky] called me a shrimp the first couple of games."

The little guy played in 82 games his rookie year, averaging 14 minutes and 8.7 points a game. Indiana won its first ABA championship, and Keller helped with some fine defense in the playoffs, particularly against Kentucky's Dampier in the first round.

All told, Billy came through his first pro season better than anyone, including himself, could have anticipated. "It's a different world," he stated, "and you don't know it until you go through it. Every player who comes into the pros was a star in college. Here, rookies have to sit on the bench while they learn to fit in. It's very difficult, probably the hardest part of being a rookie."

In his second season, 1970–71, Keller seemed like a new man. The worrying rookie was replaced by a confident—even cocky—veteran determined to show the league how good he was. In the first few weeks he averaged 22 points a game and actually led the ABA in scoring for a short while. "At the start of the year," he explained, "I was taking 18 shots a game and I was having good success hitting nine or ten. We were running, and when we run the guards score more. But of course our game is to go inside, and my job then is to set up the offense. Last year I was always in a hurry and I became impatient waiting for the plays to develop. Now, I just wait and I'm seeing more options because I have more patience."

It wasn't long before Billy moved into a starting spot, however. His scoring declined slightly as his playmaking improved. He became the envy of the rookies on the sideline.

One newcomer had an especially rough time getting his bearings. Like the old Keller, he made mistakes, got little playing time, and began to doubt his own ability. To make matters worse, this rookie

Keller gets off a bounce pass under the outstretched arms of two Utah Stars.

had signed a million-dollar contract. His name was Rick Mount.

Billy felt for his former college teammate, but was firm in his belief that coach Leonard's treatment of rookies was right. "You can learn a lot by sitting on the bench with Slick," said Keller. "I'm glad that I started the way I did. However, there were times when I became frustrated because I wanted to be in on the action. I can sympathize with Rick."

Keller's speed was particularly effective against bigger guards on offense. The Pacers were a running club, which gave the tall guards little opportunity to intimidate Billy; they were usually too busy trying to keep up with him. As the season progressed, the stocky backcourtman learned how to go inside with the ball. He would often spot an opening in the defense, get a pick or two from the Indiana giants, and flash to the bucket for a lay-up.

Early in the 1970–71 season, Indiana played Kentucky in a match that saw Keller go head-to-head with the deadliest three-point shooter in the league, Louie Dampier. On one sequence of plays, though, the two opponents seemed to exchange styles. Dampier drove at Keller, threw a head fake, and went to his left for a basket.

"Hey," Dampier yelled to Billy as he ran back on defense, "I got that move from you."

Keller didn't answer him, but when he brought the ball up, he stopped about 27 feet from the hoop and calmly tossed in a three-pointer.

"Hey, Lou," Billy laughed, "I got that one from you."

Off the court, the two eventually became close friends. On the court, their fierce duels were the talk of the ABA. Dampier was a six-footer, so their rivalry might have been termed "the War of the Mighty Mites." Billy more than held his own in the battles. He was one of the few men able to completely shut out the offense-minded Colonel star, as he had proved in his rookie playoffs.

Dampier remembered playing against Keller that season: "I knew he was awfully fast, but I didn't realize he was as good a shooter as he is. I tried to get him mad a couple of times, but he didn't even act like he heard me. I don't think I've ever been as down as I was after the playoffs, because no one had ever guarded me the way he did. Billy's as tough as there is, and I have all the respect in the world for him."

Billy also gained lots of respect for his ability to come through in the clutch. He won several games in the final moments with his foul shooting (he was one of the finest foul shooters in the ABA, averaging 87 percent over his first four years). In 1970–71, he iced a Pacer victory with four free throws in a double overtime match with Carolina. In a game with Kentucky, he hit a pair from the foul line with eight seconds remaining for another win.

When Indiana slowed down and the offense got into a rut, Billy was there to light a fire under the team. His roadrunner speed, his streak shooting and his gritty determination seemed to get his teammates moving. Billy enjoyed taking charge. "I like being a floor leader, a 'pepperpot,' " he said. "I think it's good for the team and good for the fans. The fans like to see a little guy come out on top of a big guy in anything, whether it's scoring on a fast break, grabbing a rebound or scoring a goal over the bigger defensive player."

The 1970–71 campaign was Billy's stellar year. He averaged 14.3 ppg in the regular season and 21.6 in eleven playoff matches. He established himself as one of the ABA's better three-point shots. Best of all—a tribute to his playmaking ability—he led the Pacers in both regular season and playoff assists.

The next season should have seen more of the same, but it was not to be. Keller collided with a teammate during the pre-season and suffered a badly bruised thigh. He didn't fully recover until after mid-season and didn't regain his starting spot until the 1972 playoffs.

After a November contest with the Nets, he voiced his frustration: "I'm not in the shape I have to be due to this darned thigh injury. But a guy has to learn to play with these things. Yeah, it's upsetting to know you can do the job and not play. But I'll get there. When I get my confidence I know I can beat 'em."

He had his confidence restored in time for the playoffs. He started all 20 of the post-season contests, raising his scoring from 9.7 ppg (in the regular season) to 12 ppg. He also made 40 percent of his three-point attempts. The power of those "home-run" shots was never so evident as in the fifth game of the championship round with the New York Nets. The Pacers, who trailed by 15 points at the half, roared back when the little guy fired in four shots from outside the 25-foot line. That's twelve points. Indiana won the crucial game, 100–99, and won their second ABA title in the next game.

After his good playoff showing, Billy expected to continue in his starting role in 1972–73. But the coaches felt they needed a bigger guard and they brought in Don Freeman from the Dallas Chaparrals. Freeman was 6-foot-3, a five-time All-Star, an excellent shooter and a defensive stalwart. Freeman's defensive ability was perhaps the most important to the Pacers.

There had always been questions concerning Keller's defense. Though he could, and did, have good defensive nights against fellow little men, such as Dampier and Mack Calvin, the tall guards often gave him trouble. Like other small men, Billy had to adopt special tactics to make up for his size. "If a big guard takes me inside," he explained, "I try to stay in front of him so he has to throw over my head. I also try to keep the pass away from him. I try to stay up close and harass him. I try to keep a hand on him to keep him from getting loose. This is something that comes fairly quickly after the coach tells you a few times and the opposing guys do the same to you."

But he was forced to admit: "When somebody

takes me deep under the basket, he's going to score most of the time regardless of my size."

Don Freeman's play was a major factor in Indiana's third title drive. But so was Billy Keller's. At first he was understandably unhappy about being a reserve once again. Yet, as sixth man he got ample playing time—he averaged half a game on the court. He scored in the 13-point range and was again among the leaders in foul shooting and three-pointers. Keller put the team's welfare above his own need to start, and Indiana won.

Billy was one of the most popular players ever to wear a Pacer uniform. The fans of Indianapolis loved him. He was one of their own, a hometown boy who had made good. "I want the fans to appreciate me for my ability to play basketball and help the Pacers be the best team in pro ball," said Keller. "When I first had a chance to try out with the Pacers, I worried that I might be kept just because I am from Indianapolis, or because the fans might come to see me play.

"I wanted to make the Pacers on my ability and nothing else. I know some of the veterans didn't think I could play in this league, and that made me more determined. I wanted their respect. I wanted to be one of the guys and make a contribution toward winning a championship. Every player wants to be respected by his teammates and to feel like one of the guys."

Billy Keller was one of the guys—one who helped make Indiana a super basketball team.

3. NATE ARCHIBALD

In 1972–73, Nate Archibald had one of the most remarkable seasons of any athlete in any sport. He was the first man in the history of the National Basketball Association to lead all players in both scoring average and assists in the same season, and set several other records in addition. How did he do it, people wanted to know. How could anyone so small—6-foot-1, and only 150 pounds—so completely dominate the court?

A better question might have been: how did Nate Archibald manage to keep his body, mind and spirit intact long enough to reach the NBA?

Consider that when Nate was only 14, his father left home. Nate, the oldest of seven children, became the "man" of the house. This was an awesome responsibility for one so young. Not only did he have to work (bagging groceries at a supermarket), but he had to supervise the kids and help his mother hold the family together.

Consider also that the Archibalds lived in the South Bronx, one of the ugliest, most blighted sections of New York City. Hope was a rare commodity in his neighborhood. People there had to live with crime and violence. And the use of heroin and other drugs was widespread.

One of Nate's most vivid recollections was the death of Ralph Hall. Hall was a local boy, a high school basketball hero and one of the few young men in the neighborhood to go on to college. Ahead of him lay possible All-America status and perhaps a pro career. He was 6-foot-7 and he had the potential to be great. One summer day, Hall was playing in a recreation league game. Archibald, who was still in high school, was also in the game. Hall suddenly collapsed. He was dead before an ambulance could reach him, the victim of an overdose of heroin.

The vision of Hall lying dead on the court haunted Archibald. Here was a guy who might have used his athletic skills to get away from the poverty and the drugs. "Some people have this theory," said Nate, "that when you're high you can think better, relax more, handle pressure better." Ralph Hall apparently believed that theory, and it killed him.

Nate could easily have gone that same route. Trouble usually began when groups of boys gathered on the streets because it was preferable to being inside. "Everybody lived in a project," he recalled of his neighborhood. "It was so crowded you couldn't move—four or five of us sleeping in the same room.

You'd go down to the street corner and hang around and maybe you'd drink a little or smoke."

Archibald did his share of hanging out as a youngster. He was a popular kid. His buddies called him "Tiny," short for "Little Tiny" (his father was known as "Big Tiny"). He was just one of the crowd. He had schoolyard basketball talent, but so did a lot of guys, and he didn't realize how important his talent could be until his parents split up: "I realized if I was going to make it, it would have to be in sports. I had no father and I had to work, but I was determined to make it."

His determination was nurtured by others, men like Hilton White—one of his teachers in junior high— and by Floyd Layne. During the early 1950s, Layne had been a star on a championship City College of New York team. Then Layne, along with many other players, was implicated in the practice of "fixing" games to suit gamblers and outlawed from pro basketball. Layne redeemed himself by devoting his time to community service. He ran the South Bronx's P.S. 18 Recreation Center.

"He just captured my mind," Tiny said of Layne. "Like he told me there were shower facilities at the school. Man, no one took showers. The Center opened from 7 to 10 at night. After that we'd just go home, get something to eat and go to sleep. He got us to take care of ourselves, to take care of our bodies."

Basketball was a year-round pastime at the Center. Pickup teams were composed of high school, college and pro players mixed together. The only thing that mattered was a person's ability, not his background. Tiny, at high school age, once played on a team with Em Bryant, Fred Foster, Tom Thacker and Happy Hairston. He thought they were just four good players. Later, someone told him that they were all in the pros.

Best of all, Nate had a special friend in Floyd Layne. If he had a problem, or just needed to get something off his chest, he sat down with the

Nate Archibald:
"If I was going to make it, it would have to be in sports."

ex-CCNY star. "Mr. Layne kept me off the streets,"
he said.

"Tiny's father was not home," Layne explained. "I
had to play a father role to him." Floyd did that and
more. Archibald attended DeWitt Clinton High, and
he had trouble making the basketball team there.
Clinton had about 9,000 students, and droves of them
tried out for the team. Tiny was only 5-foot-10, and
he didn't stand out. The coach couldn't give the
hopefuls a very long look; there were simply too
many. Nate caught on only briefly his junior year, but
was ultimately cut. Then Layne urged the coach to
give Archibald another chance, and the coach did.

Tiny played only one full season for Clinton, his
senior year, but that was enough. He was named to
the All-City team, and he started looking ahead. "I
figured I could go to college maybe. The only way I
was going to go was basketball. I wasn't that smart
upstairs, and I knew I had to go on scholarship. I
knew I wasn't going to go on any academic scholarship because they told me that you had to have a
foreign language and your marks had to be 80 or 90,
so that was out for me."

Archibald's bad grades frightened off plenty of
colleges. Most of them agreed that he should go to a
junior college first to prove he could do college work.
Tiny wound up at tiny Arizona Western J.C. He
concentrated on the books for one year and then
accepted a basketball scholarship from the University
of Texas at El Paso (UTEP).

Tiny broke all the scoring records at UTEP during his three years there, though he was not really a super-scorer. He averaged between 20 and 25 points per game. He was regarded as one of the outstanding players in the Western Athletic Conference, but received very little national attention. In his senior year, "Nate the Skate," as he was called because of his smooth style, assumed the additional task of playmaker, quarterbacking the Miners' complicated pattern offense.

Things went fine on the court, but Nate encountered some personal problems. First, there was a feeling of loneliness and isolation. UTEP didn't offer much social life to its black students, and the Southwest was alien to a city kid like Archibald. So when he was still a sophomore, Nate went home and married a New York girl. He brought her back to live with him on campus.

The second problem wasn't so easy to solve. While he was gone, two of his younger brothers fell prey to the ghetto streets. "It starts in the house," Archibald said. "There is nobody to supervise the older ones and the younger ones are on their own and they get into trouble. I felt for my brothers. There was nobody to help. I was away at school. I talked to them on the phone and they promised they would straighten out, they would do this and that, but if you're not there to keep on them it's hard."

Teams in both the NBA and ABA scouted him. In the spring of Archibald's senior year the NBA's

Cincinnati Royals picked him on the second round of the 1970 draft. He was chosen largely on the recommendations of the team's scouts; coach Bob Cousy had never met Tiny or seen him play. The two finally did meet under very amusing circumstances.

The story goes that Cousy and Cincinnati general manager Joe Axelson were in Memphis to see Archibald play in an all-star game following his senior year. Some time before the match, Axelson phoned Tiny and asked him to come up to his hotel room for introductions. Not long afterward, Axelson telephoned room service for some ice. There was a knock on the door a little later. It was a slender, not-very-tall young man. Axelson was just about to ask him to put the ice on the dresser when the young man said, "Hi, I'm Nate Archibald." Cousy and Axelson were stunned. At first glance they had taken Tiny for a bellhop!

It was an understandable error. In street clothes, he looked like anything but an athlete. In uniform, he gave the impression of being some kid who had taken the real Nate Archibald's place. He seemed much shorter than the 6-foot-1 at which he was listed, his scant 150 pounds made him the lightest of the little men, and a boyish face heightened the effect.

Anyway, Tiny had some proving to do. In five post-season games after his last year at UTEP, he averaged 38 points. Nate's best showing was in the Aloha Classic, held in Hawaii. As Cousy and UTEP coach Don Haskins watched from the stands, Archibald ripped the hoop for 51 points. Cousy turned to Haskins and commented that he didn't know Nate was that kind of scorer. "Well," replied the open-mouthed Haskins, "don't feel bad. I had him for three years and I didn't know it either."

One way or another, Cincinnati knew it had something special in Tiny Archibald. His size was special, certainly. He had to be fitted with a tailor-made uniform because all the available Royal outfits were too big for him. One uniform Nate never attempted to fill belonged to departed superstar Oscar Robertson. The great guard had been traded to Milwaukee after the 1969–70 season, the result of a salary dispute and his inability to get along with Bob Cousy. That left Cincy with a gap in the backcourt. But the Royals had a promising guard named Norm Van Lier. Although it seems, looking back, that Archibald had been drafted to replace Oscar, no one then expected the skinny rookie would become a superstar. Joe Axelson, however, felt Tiny could rival the "Big O" in one respect—he thought the new little man could draw spectators. "Fans identify with the little guys," he said. "This kid will put fans in the stands."

It should be noted that Archibald was not the most famous little man coming out of college in 1970. That honor went to Niagara's Calvin Murphy. Calvin joined the San Diego Rockets and got far more coverage in the newspapers. Most of the pressure to succeed rested on Murphy's shoulders—he was the

A collision between Tiny and Knick strongman Dave DeBusschere knocks both men off balance—and the ball flies free.

yardstick by which people measured the performance of the small player in the NBA. There were only a few cheering Archibald on, but at least he didn't have to contend with a legion of "experts" predicting he'd never make it.

Nate had a good pre-season, scoring 13.7 points a game and leading the club in assists. He was one of the starting guards at the beginning of the regular season. The other starting guard was six-footer Norm Van Lier. The Royals had the shortest backcourt combination in the league, but also one of the most determined.

The Royals didn't win many games, but Tiny showed his worth. He averaged 16 points (including 47 points one night against Atlanta) and five assists per game.

Tiny's rookie year was a real adventure. The first time he returned to New York City as a Royal, Cincinnati was playing the Knicks at Madison Square Garden. When Tiny attempted to enter the arena following his teammates, he was stopped by a security guard. The man thought Nate was just another kid trying to sneak in, and nothing Archibald could say or do would convince the guard otherwise. Bob Cousy had to be summoned before Tiny was finally let through. The Knicks were sorry he reached the court; he scored 19 points against them that evening.

By the end of his second pro year, everyone knew Nate Archibald. He averaged 23 points a game during the first half of the 1971–72 season, and 34 ppg for the second half. Some said he got hot late in the season because he was angry at not being named to the East squad of the NBA All-Star Game in January (he missed by one vote). Actually, Tiny took the disappointment philosophically.

No, Archibald's second-year spurt was probably due more to necessity than anger. His team needed him. Norm Van Lier had been traded early in the year, and the Royals needed someone to be their playmaker. Nate's assists average quickly picked up—he even led the league for a time—and he ended with 9.2 a game, third best in the NBA. Cincinnati also needed a scorer, so Archibald increased his shooting to fill the vacuum. The result was an overall 28.2 ppg—second highest in the league. "I've never seen a player with his assortment of shots," said an awed Bob Cousy, a man who had a pretty large assortment himself in his day. "And Nate's body balance is unbelievable. Sometimes I honestly don't see how he keeps control of himself."

Tiny had two great weapons on offense: blazing quickness and a devastating left-handed jump shot from 18 to 25 feet out. Nate could dribble downcourt faster than most players could run free. Opponents grabbed him, bumped him, tripped him, elbowed him—anything to keep him from getting past. All they did was give him foul shots. Nate took 148 more free throws than any other NBA player in '71–72.

He had some fantastic games his second year. He

had a 45-point night against the Pistons that included 23 out of 24 from the foul line. He had 49 points in a game with the Knicks and 40 points against Atlanta. Then there was the match with Portland that Cincinnati won, 110–106.

The Trail Blazers' Rick Adelman guarded—or tried to guard—Tiny in the first quarter. Archibald burned him with 17 points. Portland put rookie Charlie Yelverton on him in the second quarter with more success—Yelverton stole the ball from Tiny twice and held him to just three points. Then Adelman returned in the third stanza, and Nate feasted with 18 points. Yelverton came back in the fourth, and Archibald began scoring off him. Portland used Stan McKenzie and finally Adelman again, all to no avail. When the clubs left the court, Tiny had 55 points, six steals and seven assists.

How could anyone top Archibald's sophomore pro year? Nate himself did, the very next season. To say that he had an incredible year in 1972–73 is like saying the ocean is wet. He led the circuit in both scoring average (34 ppg) and assists (11.4 pg), to become the first NBA player ever to lead in both categories. His 910 total assists were the most ever made in one year. His was the highest scoring average and highest scoring total (2,719) ever posted by a guard. He was also the first backcourtman ever to make more than 1,000 field goals (1,028). Not only did he play in the 1973 All-Star Game and gain a berth on the All-NBA Team, but he was a runaway

Archibald gets some advice from Bob Cousy, one of the first great little men—and the coach of the Kings.

choice for the league's highest honor, the Most Valuable Player award.

Nate set all his records for a new team—the Royals had moved from Cincinnati and had become the Kansas City–Omaha Kings. If the Kings played better and drew more fans in their new homes ("home" games were divided between Missouri and Nebraska), it was largely due to the unstoppable little man from the Bronx. He was soon one of the NBA's biggest attractions, wreaking havoc wherever he played. He contributed 35 points and 15 assists in an upset victory over powerful Boston, demolished Houston with 51 points and 14 assists, and scared New York with 52 points and 15 assists in an overtime loss. That game was played in Kansas City, and the organist at the Memorial Auditorium entertained the fans with "chase" music—like that played during the old Keystone Kops movies—every time Tiny got his hands on the ball.

"It drives you crazy," the Knicks' Walt Frazier said after the game.

"Archibald or the music?" he was asked.

"Both!" was his answer.

Nate was well versed in the things he had to do to win. "There's a big difference between scoring and generating offense," he explained in the midst of his third year. "Cooz [coach Cousy] has told me he wants me to be responsible for running our offense, and to me that means I've got to create scoring opportunities—either for myself by beating the defense or for other guys by attracting the defense to me and then throwing the ball to someone they've left alone. Teams are all ganging up on me now. They're double-teaming me and playing zones and semi-zones against me. I feel the pressure, but I also know that when the pressure's on me, it's off somebody else. Then it's my job to get him the ball."

Bob Cousy had the same approach when he was a great little man back in the '50s. The coach's influence on Tiny was obvious. He said of his young star: "He has so much ability, so much speed, so much quickness. I've talked to him at length about taking charge, becoming a leader. When we're running, I want him to be the one out there who's on top of things."

Cooz did have some reservations, however: "Tiny's got a tendency to go schoolyard on you. He doesn't really discipline himself as much as he should. I was always fairly disciplined when I was playing—but then, I had nowhere near the ability to go to the basket that he does. He's so good at that, it tempts him to be a little bit loose."

Cousy left the Kings early in the 1973–74 season. At the same time, Nate was spending most of his time on the bench, the result of an injury to his right Achilles tendon. If success was measured solely in points and newsprint, then perhaps Tiny's fourth season was something of a failure. But there was more to his life than shining on the courts of the NBA.

For several years, unpaid and unpublicized, Nate

devoted his summers to coaching school kids in New York. He hoped that the influence of an NBA superstar would counteract that of the pushers and hustlers. He tried to give youngsters the kind of counsel and direction that he himself had received as a boy from men like Floyd Layne.

"Kids can identify with athletes," said Tiny. "They see you play on TV and then you come to the park and it impresses them that you care. Some of them. I try to tell them that even if they can't play in the NBA or the ABA, if they can play basketball they can get a scholarship. Then they can get a college education and become an artist or a phys ed teacher. They can become something." He was justifiably proud that by the end of 1973 a half dozen of the boys he had coached were enrolled in college.

Few men could do what Nate did, whether on a pro hardwood floor or on a cement court in a schoolyard with a bunch of admiring kids. Perhaps Bob Cousy put it best when he said, "I'd like to take credit for Tiny. I'd like to say that there's a lot of me in him, but I can't. He's all Nate Archibald. That's all there is to it. He's all his own."

4. MACK CALVIN

"When the game is close and it's about over, I want the ball because I feel I can do more for the team than anybody else."

This is how Mack Calvin characterized his approach to pro basketball. The six-foot backcourtman was the ABA's number one clutch player. As one sportswriter put it, the Carolina Cougars guard "feeds on pressure like a fat man on pastry. Pressure is Calvin's vitamin pill. It makes him feel better."

Pressure? Imagine being on the foul line with the score tied and four seconds to go in the game. That was the situation in one match between Carolina and Eastern Division rival Kentucky. Despite a pulled hamstring muscle, Calvin was enjoying a good game. But it was a tough scrap, with neither team dominating.

On one play, Carolina's Billy Cunningham had rebounded a missed shot and hit Calvin—who was leading the fast break—with a long pass. Kentucky had gotten back quickly on defense; with barely a moment to take his shot before the end of the third quarter, Mack found his path to the basket blocked by Colonels. Mack faked to his right, dribbled behind his back, went left, and pulled up at the three-point line, 25 feet from the hoop. The buzzer sounded just as he released his jump shot. The red, white and blue ABA ball arced smoothly—and fell through the net. Three points!

The teams continued to battle late into the last quarter with the lead seesawing back and forth. Then, with ten seconds left, Kentucky's little man, Louie Dampier—another good player in the clutch—tied the game, 112–all. After calling a time-out, the Cougars inbounded the ball to Calvin, who raced for the hoop. Suddenly, the Colonels' tremendous center, 7-foot-2 Artis Gilmore, came over to stop the sure two points. He succeeded. Mack tripped over Gilmore's feet and went head over heels to the floor. Gilmore was called for a foul.

Mack went to the free-throw line with just four seconds on the game clock. A hushed silence fell over the partisan Carolina crowd. Calvin bounced the ball a few times, took a deep breath and let fly. Swish! The score was 113–112, Carolina. He got the ball back for his second attempt. Mack's forehead wrinkled with concentration. Again the ball went up. Swish! The Cougars led, 114–112, and that's the way the game ended.

"I like to be in a situation like that," Calvin

explained later in the locker room. "I was going to the hoop all the way and had my man beat. I don't think Artis meant to foul me, but it was a good foul, because I would have had two points.

"I was stinging all over from the fall, but I just had to shake it off. The pressure was on the first free throw. I had to make that one because if I missed it and hit the second, they had a chance to win. But I had confidence that both shots would go in."

It was difficult to find a more confident athlete when the heat was on. When Mack was a senior at the University of Southern California, he took a test administered by a team of psychologists at San Jose State College.

"It was to determine how you could handle pressure in tight situations," Calvin recalled. "A total of 15,000 high school, college and pro athletes took it. I scored the highest. The psychologists thought I could handle the pressure better than anyone."

Bob Boyd, Mack's basketball coach at USC, elaborated on the results: "The test tells you about a player's talent for winning, about how he will react under adverse circumstances. It tells you about how much of a player's physical ability he can give you when the situation is the toughest. The men who administered the test had no idea if Calvin was two feet tall or eight feet tall. They just said that the tougher the situation, the better this guy likes it."

Until Mack sat down with the test, the man with the highest score was Billy Kilmer, later the fiery

Starring for USC in 1968, Mack Calvin leaps up to grab a rebound from a taller UCLA opponent. Abdul-Jabbar (then Lew Alcindor) watches at left.

quarterback of the NFL's Washington Redskins. That Calvin could beat out a super-competitor like Kilmer was sure indication of the little man's spirit.

Mack Calvin was born in Fort Worth, Texas, in 1948. While he was still a toddler, his family moved to Long Beach, California. Mack was a natural athlete. As a youngster, he spent the fall and winter playing basketball and devoted his spring and summer to baseball. He was the star playmaker on Long Beach Poly High School's basketball squad. The team lost only four games in his three years on the varsity. In baseball he was an outstanding shortstop.

Like many multi-talented athletes, he was faced with a hard decision upon his graduation. The Los Angeles Dodgers offered him good money to play baseball, but Calvin liked basketball, too, and he wanted to further his education. He enrolled at a local school, Long Beach Junior College, to think it out.

Baseball came in second. Southern Cal wanted him on its basketball team and was willing to offer a scholarship. So, at the end of his two junior college years, Calvin dropped all thoughts of a baseball career to join USC.

Coach Bob Boyd's Trojan basketball team was overshadowed by its crosstown rival, UCLA. But the Trojans did have two winning seasons with Calvin as their floor leader. Mack established a reputation as a fair scorer and a fearless ballhandler. One of his valued possessions was a photograph of him driving on Lew Alcindor (later known as Kareem Abdul-Jabbar), UCLA's giant super-center.

For a time, it looked as if the only thing he couldn't do was get on a pro basketball team. Apparently the scouts from the two leagues weren't very impressed with him. The major factor was, of course, his lack of height. In 1969 there were very few men under 6-foot-2 in either the NBA or ABA, and the pro teams were not much inclined to gamble on a small player.

Bob Boyd almost had to beg the Los Angeles Stars of the ABA to give Calvin a chance. They finally agreed, drafting him on the seventh round behind more than 50 other players. In the NBA, no one mentioned Calvin until the 14th round, when he was picked by the Los Angeles Lakers. The higher the round, the better the chance of making the team. Pro coaches always paid more attention to their early-draft rookies in training camp. Usually only two or three rookies ever made the squad.

Mack reasoned that his best chance was with the Stars. The Lakers simply had too much talent in the backcourt for an unknown little man to crack the line-up. He fit right in with the Stars; the only well-known face on the team belonged to Bill Sharman—the coach.

The Stars were a very young, very unsettled team. They seemed to field a different line-up every game. "We had so many injuries that things were impossible," remembered Calvin. "And there were so many trades, there appeared to be a new guy coming in every week."

Calvin managed to hold his own throughout the chaos. He played in every game—usually starting—and finished the regular season second in league assists and scored 16.8 points per game. Teammates gave him the nickname "Mack the Knife," for his ability to slash defenses apart.

The "Knife" was even sharper in the 1970 playoffs. Surprisingly, the ungainly Stars drove all the way to the championship series, there to be defeated in six games by a powerhouse Indiana club. In the 19 post-season contests, Mack cut his opponents at a rate of 23.1 points a game. He easily made the ABA's All-Rookie team.

Calvin would have liked to play his entire pro career in Los Angeles, but that was not to be. The city could not support two big-league teams. The established Lakers, featuring superstars Wilt Chamberlain, Jerry West and Elgin Baylor, played to packed houses while the Stars had to make do with those fans who couldn't get Laker tickets. "We had too many crowds of 900," recalled Calvin.

At the close of Mack's rookie year (1969–70) his club moved to Salt Lake City to become the Utah Stars. Calvin never made the trip; he and forward Tom Washington were traded to the Miami Floridians for All-Star guard Don Freeman and a draft choice.

His new club was another team in transition. It had

lost so many games in 1969–70 that the ownership decided some drastic changes were needed. First, in a startling turnabout, the coach kept his job, but the entire team was "fired." Every player on the 1969–70 roster was either cut or traded before the next season. Second, in an effort to increase attendance, the team dropped the "Miami" from its name and simply became the Floridians, a regional franchise playing in Miami, Tampa, Jacksonville and several other cities around the state. Third, and most significant to Calvin, the team planned to make him the key player on the squad.

For all their wheeling and dealing, the Floridians couldn't come up with a really good big man, so coach Hal Blitman (the man whose job was spared) reasoned that the team could only win with a running attack and plenty of outside shooting. What better player to lead that attack than Mack Calvin, one of the quickest men in the ABA?

Blitman's plan didn't quite work. Calvin ran the show, and the team ran against its opponents, but the Floridians wound up on the short end in the win-loss column. Most of the scoring came out of the back-court. Mack and fellow guard Larry Jones contributed over 50 points a game between them. But the frontcourt and the reserves had trouble playing defense, rebounding and scoring. The result was 18 wins and 30 losses in the first half of 1970–71. Blitman, a man Mack greatly respected, was fired.

Bob Bass, Blitman's replacement, came in with

Carolina's Calvin gets past Bill Schaffer of the Nets for the two-pointer.

entirely different ideas. He felt the team should slow down and play a deliberate, pattern offense. This meant bringing the ball up slowly and passing it from man to man until one player finally took a shot. The new plan completely nullified Calvin's greatest asset, his lightning speed. Still, he ended up with a 27.1-point average (fourth best in the league) and made 7.6 assists per game (second best). The Floridians had a 37–47 record and were eliminated in the first playoff round, but in those six games Mack averaged better than 23 points. It was his finest year as a pro.

The following season, 1971–72, the Floridians did worse: a 36–48 record. The college draft hadn't added much talent, there was dissension on the squad, and even fewer people than before came out to see the team. Some players—Calvin among them—felt that the owners could have gotten some top talent had they been willing to spend big money on a super rookie like Artis Gilmore, who played his college ball at Jacksonville, or a superstar veteran like Rick Barry, who had played at the University of Miami. Everyone was dissatisfied and apathy prevailed. "Nobody cared whether you won or lost," Calvin said.

Mack once again led the team in scoring (21 per game) and assists (5). But he admitted he didn't give it his all that season: "The first year I didn't let it bug me, although I wanted to get out. But the second year was the worst. All of a sudden I wasn't trying like I used to. I lost a little bit of my love for the game."

The Floridians, along with the Pittsburgh Condors —two clubs that were financial disasters—were dissolved after the '71–72 season. The players on both teams were drafted by the remaining ABA teams. Mack was snatched up by the Carolina Cougars, which suited him just fine. "I'm glad the Floridians folded," he said after he had negotiated his Carolina contract. "I would never have gone back. Never. I'm really excited to be with the Cougars. I see players who want to try. I see a team that can win and knows it can. I see fans who will come out and support you."

Like the Floridians, the Cougars were a regional franchise, playing their home games in various cities in their state (North Carolina). But there the resemblance ended. Carolina's team—which included former NBA stars Billy Cunningham and Joe Caldwell—was far superior to any that Mack had played on. Although they had never won a title, the Cougars had the potential, especially with the addition of Mack Calvin.

Carolina had a new coach, Larry Brown, who had set all kinds of playmaking records when he was an active player in the league. At 5-foot-9, 160 pounds, Larry was one of the smallest men ever to play in the pros, and no doubt he saw a lot of himself in Calvin. Brown was an innovator. The first thing he did was to install a running offense and a full-court trapping defense. Mack fit right in. "I've played that way all my life," the Knife said. "My role has always been to get things in motion and to control the break, which I

Net Tom Washington intercepts a pass intended for Calvin, but the little Cougar gets a hand in and forces a jump ball.

like to do. And also to play hard-nosed defense."

Yes indeed, Mack did play hard-nosed defense. But Brown's concept of defense caused a great deal of confusion in training camp. The Carolina guards, as the coach saw it, would harass their opponents from baseline to baseline. They would pin the enemy ballhandler against a side line, double-team him and hope for an interception or a steal. This aggressive defense coupled with a fast-breaking offense would quickly tire the Cougar backcourtmen, Brown thought. They couldn't possibly play a whole game at full tilt. So, Brown experimented with a platoon system. Starting guards Calvin and Steve Jones would frequently be relieved by Ted McClain and Gene Littles. Each set of guards would play about half the game.

Calvin didn't think the system would work. He felt Brown would soon abandon it. But the Cougars won their first four games in 1972–73, and the coach was pleased with his experiment. It was, after all, a system that no other team in pro basketball used.

But Mack was still less than enthusiastic: "It bothered me somewhat, not playing that much. I never before had been in a situation when I didn't play 35 to 40 minutes. And here I was playing a lot less. I'd find myself on the bench thinking I should be playing in tight situations. After a loss, I would think if I played more, things might have been different."

He had a private session with his coach to make his complaint. Brown convinced him to stick with it. By mid-season, Carolina had the best record in the ABA: 37 wins, 16 losses. "I can't knock the system now," Mack smiled. "Winning takes away a lot of selfishness."

Calvin learned how to make the most of his abbreviated playing time. One of his favorite drills, one he practiced every day, was to dribble the ball for exactly three seconds and shoot. One . . . two . . . three . . . shoot. The drill taught him to keep the ball moving whether he was scoring or whipping quick passes to his teammates. There was a game against Memphis in which he hit six consecutive jump shots in the third quarter. He went to the showers after the game with 31 points in 31 minutes of play. Opponents around the league grimaced every time he got his hands on the ball. "Calvin not only scores," sighed New York's John Roche, "he makes you look stupid doing it."

Calvin was named to the East squad for the 1973 All-Star Game. It was the third time he had played in the classic, but this time it held far more significance. Although he had less playing time than any other backcourtman named to the team, he still was the top vote-getter among the East guards. "I guess that is the most satisfying thing ever to happen to me in basketball," he commented. "Being recognized by the other players, the coaches, and the media. Realizing they could see that what I was doing was important."

The reduced court time naturally lowered Calvin's statistics. At the end of his first year with the Cougars, he had scored 17.5 points per game in the regular season and 18.2 in 12 playoff matches. His assists were lower, too. Still, taking his first four years in the ABA, he had made substantial dents in the record book. In regular-season play he ranked among the league leaders in scoring average, assists, free throws attempted and made, free-throw average (86 percent) and total points (6,808). In playoff action, he ranked high in scoring average, total points and assists.

Statistics, no matter how glowing, are meaningless when you lose. The 1972–73 Cougars were winners. No, they didn't win a championship—they were stopped by Kentucky in the semifinal playoffs—but Carolina did finish in first place in their division with what was then the finest record ever posted by an ABA club, 57–27. The Cougars, with Calvin's aid, established themselves as a team to be reckoned with in the coming years.

"I've never been happier playing basketball," said the little man from Long Beach. "Winning does make all the difference. I've always felt inside I'm a winner. Now I'm on a winning team again."

5. LOUIE DAMPIER

When the ABA was formed in 1967, the association's owners knew their enterprise had to have innovations that would set the new league apart from the established NBA and hopefully bring in the fans. Among other things, they introduced a red, white and blue ball, a 30-second shot clock (the NBA's ran 24 seconds) and the controversial three-point basket.

Awarding three points for a basket from 25 feet or more—the so-called home-run shot—gave good outside shooters a powerful new weapon. But only a handful learned to be consistent with it. The best of the breed was Louie Dampier, a guard for the Kentucky Colonels who may turn out to be the finest three-point shooter ever. Over his first six years in the ABA, he made 676 of the special shots, 231 more than his nearest rival. In 1968–69 he tossed in a record 199 home runs, and in six seasons he scored on 35 percent of his long shots.

A three-point shooter could bring his team from

behind in a big hurry. If he was fouled in the act of shooting a successful three-pointer, he could score four or even five points in a single play. Although the new scoring system added a novel element of excitement, some fans felt it violated the basic concept of basketball—to work the ball inside for a good shot.

When questioned about this, Louie Dampier replied indignantly: "I can only be concerned with whether I'm helping or hurting my team—not with the nature of basketball. If I take a hundred shots and hit my 36 percent, that's worth 108 points. If the 50 percent shooter takes a hundred shots closer in, he's only going to get 100 points. If I'm hurting anybody, it's the opposition.

"And the home-run shot adds to the game in another way," he continued. "Every time a guy hits one, it seems to give his team a lift far beyond the extra point value. It's like the start of a rally and it gets everyone's adrenalin flowing.

"Beyond that," said the Colonel guard, "the three-point basket means more to me personally than it does to most other players in the league. I'm a little guy, six feet, and I can't go in all the way against the big fellas. This way, the defense has to come out and get me beyond the 25-foot mark, and then I can beat them in for the 15-foot jump shot. Without the home-run line, they'd play me back and pick me up at the 20-foot mark. If I beat 'em from there, I'm in too close to the big man to get off a good shot. It means a lot to me."

Louie meant a lot to the Colonels and to the ABA. He was much more than simply a long-distance shooter. Dampier was one of the steadiest, most durable players in the league. Leader, gunner, playmaker, defender—he was everything to his team.

At the start of the 1973–74 season, Dampier was one of only a handful of players who had been in the league since its beginning, and he was the last of the original Colonels. No man in the ABA had more minutes of playing time, over 19,000, the equivalent of 400 full games.

Drafted in 1967 out of the University of Kentucky, Louie became a starter early in his rookie year. He never relinquished his backcourt spot, no matter how many changes the team made in personnel, coaches and playing styles. In their early seasons the Colonels were weak in the frontcourt, so the scoring punch had to come from the guards. Louie gave Kentucky 20.7, 24.8 and 26 points-per-game scoring averages his first three regular seasons, following with 26.6, 22.3 and 17.7 in playoffs those years.

Usually, a player must adapt to his team's way of doing things, but with the formative Colonels it was the other way around—Kentucky molded itself to the talents of Dampier and fellow guard Darel Carrier. Neither man was particularly fast, which meant the team couldn't run very often. Instead, the Colonels used patterns to set up their deadeye backcourt. The big guys were there to set picks and screens for Louie and Darel. Both men were sure shots from anywhere

Dampier fights for the ball with Oakland's Warren Armstrong in a 1967 game.

on the court, especially from 15 feet and out. The guards accounted for more than half the club's scoring.

Even though Kentucky was then a mediocre club, Dampier's early pro years were personally gratifying. He was an All-Star almost every year, and he had earned the reputation of a tough competitor. The Louisville fans liked him not just because he was a graduate of the University of Kentucky, but because of his gritty spirit.

For all his success, it wasn't a matter of instant stardom. His game was weak in certain areas. He hadn't been a great ballhandler in college, and this deficiency was evident when he reached the big time. And he had a tendency to stand around when he was without the ball. Since he was quickly thrust into a starting role (principally due to his shooting prowess), he had to learn the basics of playmaking in the heat of battle.

Louie recognized his shortcomings. His improvement was noticeable over the years. "Dampier is getting a lot better," said coach Gene Rhodes during the little man's third season (1969–70). "He was having problems adjusting to the pros. He was crying a lot.

"They're hitting you, holding you, nudging you," Rhodes elaborated. "It's a lot different than in college. He knows how to get open now. They won't let you get the ball here. You have to move without the ball."

His periodic troubles aside, Dampier soon established himself as an outside shooter to be feared. In one 1969 match, he set a club record, scoring on nine three-pointers in eleven attempts. One year later he scored 55 points against Dallas while setting a team mark for most total field goals made in a single game—19 two-pointers and four three-pointers. Another team record was the 25 (of 76) home-run baskets he scored in twelve playoff games in 1970.

The young Colonels depended heavily on Louie's hot hand. It wasn't until later that Kentucky added a new dimension to its offense with high-quality big men. University of Kentucky star Dan Issel came in 1970 and a year later was joined by 7-foot-2 center Artis Gilmore. The emphasis then shifted inside, and Dampier's job was to see that they got the ball. His scoring averages dropped accordingly, and for the first time since he began playing the game, people weren't looking for him to be the top gun.

Louie had first started gunning back in his hometown, Indianapolis, Indiana. While he was a star at Southport High School, his uncanny shooting ability came to the attention of Adolph Rupp, the long-time coach of the University of Kentucky Wildcats. Rupp, also known as "the Baron," was used to hearing exaggerations about spectacular young players across the nation, so he had to be persuaded to take a look at this little kid who was supposedly turning games inside-out with his long jumpers.

The story goes that Rupp climbed into his car and

drove from Lexington (home of the university) to Indianapolis for one of Southport's games. Ordinarily, the Baron would watch a recruiting prospect for a whole game or more before he would make a decision. This time, Rupp sat through the first half of the Southport game and then he left. He was satisfied: he wanted this boy Dampier in a Wildcat uniform.

And Lou wanted just as much to be in that uniform once Rupp approached him. Kentucky had a glowing basketball history, and the old coach was perhaps the most respected mentor in the college game. When the Baron offered an athletic scholarship, Louie accepted happily.

It wasn't easy playing for Baron Rupp. The coach was irritable, dictatorial and all business in his approach to the game. You played basketball his way or not at all. His domineering ways seemed unnecessarily harsh to some, but they were undeniably successful—a long string of Southeast Conference titles and national rankings attest to that. Prior to 1966, Rupp had been named college Coach of the Year three times.

Although they were not close, Louie experienced little difficulty getting used to the old man. "I think one of the secrets of his success is that he always has his players playing scared," Dampier explained a few years after he finished at the university. "He's so serious about everything. You get scared into playing good. It wasn't so bad for me because I had a coach

Playing for the University of Kentucky in 1966, Dampier shoots over two Tennessee rivals.

in high school like that. Coach Rupp has his players' minds on the game all the time."

The Baron never allowed a player to contradict him, even when the player was in the right. Louie found that out the hard way. During a defensive drill, Rupp began to yell at him. The player Louie was covering kept getting away from him. Finally, Dampier had had enough. "I got tired of catching hell," he remembered. "Another man wasn't switching with me. So, I told Rupp it wasn't my fault."

Rupp blinked, turned red in the face and glared at Dampier. "You don't talk back to me," he growled. "Go take a shower!" Louie took a shower.

Louie's sophomore year, his first on the varsity, the Wildcats limped to a poor 15–10 record. Voices were raised calling for Rupp to resign. But he stayed on, and everyone in Lexington was happy he did.

The next season was sweet. Kentucky barreled to a 27–2 record, advancing all the way to the finals of the NCAA championship before losing to Texas Western (now the University of Texas at El Paso). The Wildcats were the second best team in the country and Rupp took his fourth Coach of the Year award. The season was all the more impressive because not one of the Kentucky starters was taller than 6-foot-5, earning them the nickname "Rupp's Runts." Dampier himself gained All-America honors.

Kentucky was eager for the 1966–67 season. Preseason polls had them tabbed as strong contenders for the number one spot in college ball, but this was not to be. A key starter, Pat Riley, got injured before the start of the season and the Wildcats struggled without him. Even Louie's fine shooting couldn't put things together. The best the team could manage was a 13–13 record, the worst for Rupp in over 30 years at Kentucky.

While Louie was playing his disappointing senior year, the ABA was still in the planning stage. It was decided that Louisville should have a franchise, and the owners of that club began casting around for talent. The first place they looked was in their own backyard, various college teams in the state. Their top choice in the draft was Louie Dampier.

He came to the Colonels with strong credentials. The Baron had called him the "greatest basket shooter" he'd ever coached. Louie had made over 50 percent of his shots in his 80 varsity games. (Rupp was famous for his low opinion of pro basketball, yet when he retired as a coach he followed Louie to the Kentucky Colonels as vice-chairman of the Board of Directors.)

Louie did just fine in his early years with the Colonels. Some critics argued that that was due to the fact he didn't have to be an outstanding playmaker. What would happen, they asked, if the club's shooting personnel improved and he had to handle the ball much more often?

That question was answered in the 1970s, when Dan Issel and Artis Gilmore entered the picture. With these two on the roster, Dampier was no longer the Colonels' central figure. Issel and Gilmore shouldered much of the point-making, and Kentucky's offense became faster and looser than it had been in previous years. Suddenly, the accent was on the inside game.

Dampier erased any doubts concerning his ability —or willingness—to give up the ball during the 1970–71 season. He had 460 assists (sixth highest in

Dampier streaks past the New York Nets' Julius Erving during the 1974 playoffs.

the league). Rookie Dan Issel was on the receiving end of most of those passes. With Louie's aid, the young big man led the ABA in scoring with almost 30 points a game. Louie's own scoring fell to 18.5 ppg.

But the '70–71 regular season was just a warmup for Dampier. In the initial playoff round, in a game with the Floridians, he set an ABA record with 18 assists. Kentucky made it all the way to the championship round, where it battled Utah even for six matches before losing the seventh and decisive game. Louie hadn't forgotten how to shoot—in the fourth game of the finals he scored 33, including two crucial free throws in the waning seconds to win for Kentucky—but he caught even more attention with his playmaking. When the 1971 playoffs were over, Dampier had totaled an incredible 179 assists in 19 games—that's better than nine a game—topping the old ABA playoff record by 50.

He continued to refute his critics the following years. He had 515 assists in 1971–72 and 521 (fourth best in the league) in 1972–73. At the end of the 1973–74 season, he ranked third in playmaking. He had more total assists (3,128 at the end of '73–74) than any man in the league.

No player in the ABA ranked so high in so many lifetime categories as Dampier. Again, by the close of the '72–73 he was first in all-time minutes played, first in three-point field goals attempted and made, second in most points (9,771, behind Indiana's Mel Daniels), fourth in three-point field-goal percentage, fourth in most games played (479), eighth in two-point field goals attempted, tenth in scoring average (20.4 ppg in six years), tenth in free-throw percentage (.82) and tenth in free throws made (1,827). He also held the pro basketball record for consecutive free throws made: 58 in 1970–71.

But cold statistics can't really tell what kind of player he was. You had to watch him in action. There was a game in January 1973 when Louie went for his 10,000th point. He needed 18 points to reach that prestigious level on his home court, since the Colonels' next game was away. No one, least of all the enthusiastic Louisville fans, could have blamed him for gunning the ball. Instead, he chose to pass off, and Kentucky beat the Stars, 115–106. Dampier finished the game with 10 assists and 17 points, one short of what he needed. He had postponed his personal glory for the good of the team.

That was the kind of player Louie Dampier was.

6. NORM VAN LIER

If Norm Van Lier had taken up boxing, he might have been a contender for the light-heavyweight title. Instead, he became a little man for basketball's Chicago Bulls—one of the toughest little men in the game. One writer observed: "Van Lier spends more time on the ground than any other player in the league. His favorite trick is to get in front of a fast-breaking opponent, hoping for an offensive foul. Sometimes it works. Sometimes it doesn't. Always it hurts."

Norm's habit of throwing his body at enemy players, on both offense and defense, led to any number of fist fights. Since he was only 6-foot-1 and 175 pounds, more often than not his adversaries were much bigger men. Fans still talk about the night he challenged 7-foot-2, 280-pound Wilt Chamberlain to a fight. Luckily, none of Wilt's punches landed, and the dispute was quickly broken up. But it demonstrated one thing—Van Lier wasn't going to back down for any man.

"You've got to take a stand," the Chicago Bulls guard explained. "If you're small, they'll take it out on you all the time. I'm not going to take that. I'll get back some way, if I have to go get a folding chair."

Van Lier never had to use a folding chair, and the fights—though heavily publicized—were not the central part of his career. What he did best, the things that really gave his opponents headaches, was to guide the Chicago offense and play fine defense. Playmaking and defense may not be as attention-getting as brawling, but they do win ball games. And Norm's prowess in those two areas won plenty of games for the Bulls.

The irony of it was that he played for Chicago at all. Although the Bulls originally drafted him, they traded him to another team before he could play one regular-season game. It was only after he had two outstanding seasons with Cincinnati that the Bulls' management realized their mistake and succeeded in getting him back.

Van Lier wasn't very famous when he first entered the NBA, but a few years earlier, along about 1965, he was known as one of the best all-round high school athletes in the nation. Norm grew up in the town of Midland, Pennsylvania, the son of a steelworker. He took an early interest in several sports, especially football. A good throwing arm marked him as a starting quarterback on the Midland High football squad. He also possessed speed and a willingness to hit people hard, so naturally he found himself playing defensive back, too. He intercepted 13 passes his senior year.

Norm was a star shortstop on the Midland baseball team. The first, and only, time he ran the 100-yard dash for his school he was timed at ten seconds flat.

He was the high scorer and backcourt leader of Midland's basketball team. Van Lier worked hard to perfect his skills. One of his favorite drills was to .go outside, find a bunch of younger boys, and dribble the ball around while they attempted to steal it away from him. He got the idea from a story about Jerry West, the Lakers' All-Star guard. The long hours of practice paid off. Midland, with Van Lier running the show, won the state championship in 1965.

After the excitement died down, Norm was faced with some very hard decisions. Baseball's St. Louis Cardinals wanted him to skip college and sign up with their organization. The University of Nebraska urged him to accept a football scholarship. There were numerous offers to play college basketball.

Norm's mother wanted him to go to college. That left basketball and football. Football was his favorite, but he began to have doubts about his size. Nebraska played in the Big Eight Conference, where the athletes were almost as big as those in the National Football League. He wasn't afraid of getting hurt, only of having to sit on the bench.

"All this left me thoroughly confused," he recalled, "so I went to my high school coach for advice. He told me to get an education, not to worry about pro

Norm Van Lier: "If you're small, they'll take it out on you all the time."

ball, and if I got the opportunity, then I would get the opportunity."

He eventually settled on St. Francis College, a small school located in Loretto, Pennsylvania. St. Francis offered a sound academic program and fielded strong basketball teams. Maurice Stokes, an NBA star of the 1950s, was an alumnus of the school.

St. Francis and Norm Van Lier were made for each other. He received the education so important to his mother and coach. Norm majored in history, while minoring in social science.

During Norm's three varsity years, the college's basketball teams weren't very tall. In fact, he played most of the time at forward, since there were men even shorter than he to play in the backcourt. Van Lier averaged 18.8 points per game in that three-year period. Remarkably, he set a school record with 293 assists from his frontcourt position in his senior year.

Those were happy years for the kid from Midland. But there were bad times, too. One day in 1966 his best friend was hit by an automobile. When Van Lier got the news that his buddy had died in the hospital, he was so stricken he put his hand through a window. The next day St. Francis had a game. Norm played because he owed it to the team and because it was better to be on the court than home overcome with grief. He played despite the 33 stitches in his right hand. That's the kind of person he was.

Norm was picked on the third round of the 1969 college draft by the Chicago Bulls. The Chicago management felt they were taking a chance picking him even that high. His height, of course, was against him. Could he penetrate defenses to confront bruising big men? What about his defense? Stopping your opponent is the name of the game in the NBA. What would happen when Van Lier had to cover one of the many tall guards in the league? On top of all this, Chicago had some doubts concerning his ability to score.

He didn't have a big name when he joined the Bulls' fall training camp. He was just another rookie hopeful, and a short one at that. Norm simply did the things he did best. He survived cuts, though he wasn't given much of a chance to show his talents in the exhibition games. During those matches, Van Lier found himself on the bench, behind one of the starters. "I really got just one chance at Chicago," he explained, "and that lasted only two games when Jerry Sloan got sick."

Those two games changed his career. Fate decreed that both were against the Cincinnati Royals. Royals coach Bob Cousy was looking for a young, quick, playmaking guard, and Van Lier fit the bill. Not long afterward, Cincinnati proposed a trade, offering Walt Wesley (a back-up center, something the Bulls needed badly) and a future draft choice for Van Lier and another player. It was a deal.

Van Lier had mixed emotions about the trade. Sure, he wanted a chance to play. But Cincinnati featured superstar Oscar Robertson in the backcourt, a man who was used to leading his team in both scoring and assists. The guards who teamed with the "Big O" usually ran around with little to do, at least on offense. Then too, some Cincinnati sportswriters openly questioned Norm's ability.

If Norm had any self-doubts, he kept them well hidden. In fact, he came on as cocky. "I think these veterans have it all backwards," he told a sportswriter the very first week he joined the Royals. "I think they should worry about me, instead of me worrying about them. I'm here to make it, and a superstar is going to have to prove to me that he's better."

Tough words for a rookie—especially for a short, virtually unknown rookie. And, those words took on added meaning because he was warning both opponents and teammates.

But nothing could quite prepare the NBA for Norm Van Lier. By the end of the 1969–70 season, he had earned the nickname "Norm the Storm" for his ferocious play. He had committed a total of 329 personal fouls—the most on his team—and fouled out of 18 games, more than any other player in the NBA that year.

Despite his penchant for fouling, Norm proved a valuable asset to the Royals. From the very start of his rookie season, he got loads of playing time. By the middle of the year, Van Lier was a regular in the lineup. In fact, Norm played a total of 2,895 minutes, more than any other Royal including Robertson.

Shooting certainly wasn't his strong point. Norm

averaged a mere 9.5 points per game, and he made only 40 percent of the field goals he attempted—lowest among the regulars. On another NBA team, Norm's weak shooting might have kept him on the bench, but not on coach Bob Cousy's squad.

When a reporter asked the coach why he played Van Lier as much as he did, Cousy replied: "The way this kid hustles, he has to be in the lineup somewhere."

Cousy, an NBA superstar during the 1950s, felt a special kinship with his young guard. The premier little man of his day, Cousy had been just about the same size as Van Lier and had played the same kind of ball. Although the coach had also been one of the finest shooting guards in the league's history, Cousy could see a bit of himself in Van Lier's ability to hit the open man with quick, sure passes and in his iron defense.

Cousy was Norm's biggest cheerleader. He once said of Van Lier: "His instinct for the game and his anticipation are his strongest attributes. His constant, sustained hustle makes up for a lot of things. He rebounds exceptionally well for his size and isn't afraid to go in there with the big guys. And he jumps in and draws the charging foul as well as anyone I've ever seen in this league."

Norm felt a mutual admiration for his boss. "There's always been a question of me being too small," he said, "but Cousy gave me confidence. And

Playing for Cincinnati in 1969, Norm knocks the ball away from Warrior Clyde Lee.

it's worth it to me to get a few bruises and hustle like hell for the man who gave me my chance. There is a place for the little guy in this league."

The 1970–71 Royals were a changed team. Oscar Robertson was gone, traded to the Milwaukee Bucks. Cousy wanted more balanced scoring from his relatively young team. With the "Big O" absent, Van Lier took Robertson's place as the club's backcourt leader. His new partner was a rookie named Nate Archibald.

"Van Lier is playing now like he did most of the last half of the year," commented Cousy early in the season. "He has the confidence and the experience and he's running the show. They'll be looking for him this year. A lot of people didn't take him seriously, but this year with the defense looking for him, it could be a different story."

Norm faced his new, frightening role realistically. "My coach has confidence in me. That helps. I'm never going to be a big scorer. My job is to play defense and make assists. If I make a lot of assists, we win.

"This year my man is going to have to work to make two points. I want to shut them out and if I can't do that, I want to hold them under their average."

Van Lier went on to have a simply super year. He did everything for his team but sell popcorn. He logged more playing time (appearing in all 82 games) than any man on the club. There was no better playmaker in the entire league; Norm averaged 10.1

assists per game, tops in the NBA. Wonder of wonders, he scored a more-than-respectable 16 points a game and made 81 percent of his free throws. And, though he led the league in personal fouls, he was only tossed out of 12 games during his second pro year.

He got off to a good start in 1971–72, but he was destined to finish the year in another uniform. The Royals were in desperate need of a center. The man they wanted was Jim Fox of the Chicago Bulls. Chicago, in turn, saw a chance to remedy a big mistake, trading away Norm. So in October 1971, Van Lier found himself back with the Bulls.

Norm was a happy man. Chicago, with his help, made it to the playoffs that year. Along the way, he finally received due recognition for his solid defense, being named to the prestigious NBA All-Defense team. He also finished sixth in league assists.

The following season, '72–73, he failed to be voted to the West squad for the NBA All-Star game, held in January. He felt he deserved the honor, but instead of brooding over it, he played all the harder. His assists increased, and so did the bumps, bruises and fights.

One night, in a game against the Atlanta Hawks, Norm waged a kind of personal battle with Hawk center Walt Bellamy. Time after time, Van Lier drove inside, confronting the 6-foot-11 pivot man. The two collided with bone-crunching force once, twice, three times. With every hit, Norm went down with a crash. Each time, he jumped to his feet and when he got the

This time Van Lier shows a little too much hustle guarding Bullet Kevin Porter.

ball back, took the battle again to his opponent. Then Van Lier hit the wood floor a fourth time, the result of a Bellamy forearm. When he got up, blood was streaming down his face from a gash above his eye. Another man might have called it quits—his coach urged him to take a rest—but Norm sat down just long enough to get his wound patched, and went back in.

"You really get used to playing with pain," he said

later on. "The only guy who tries to hurt me is Walt Bellamy. If I'm pestering those big guys, they're going to be upset. But nobody does it like Bellamy. I watch for it every game. He's trying to hurt me for real."

He collected plenty of cuts and scrapes. If they were the result of diving for a loose ball, or grabbing for a rebound, so be it. But if an opponent intentionally fouled him, Norm often retaliated with his fists. Even the officials weren't safe from his wrath. Van Lier once threw a punch at a referee who was attempting to break up a fight between Norm and another player. Another time, he became angry at an official's call and threw a basketball at the man.

"I don't get a fair shake," he complained. "They protect the superstars. I have to handle every superstar that comes in and he's going to the foul line all the time, and I'm leading the league in fouls and getting thrown out of every game."

He ended up fifth in NBA assists (7.1 per game) in '72–73. In his first four years in the league he had finished ninth, first, sixth and fifth in playmaking. These are more than numbers; these are a tangible tribute to his hustle. No wonder Van Lier's favorite sports star is Pete Rose of baseball's Cincinnati Reds. Rose is known as "Charlie Hustle."

A writer once asked Norm how long he could play his exhausting, aggressive game. Van Lier replied, "Every game, the whole schedule, every season. I'm young and I'm gonna play this way until I'm too old to do it."

7. FREDDIE LEWIS

The life of a pro basketball player isn't all bright lights, standing ovations and pats on the back. Just ask Freddie Lewis. The Indiana Pacers' captain knew what it was to suffer through long nights of vocal criticism from the hometown fans. During his first six years with the Pacers, he often received warmer greetings on opposing courts than he did at home in Indianapolis.

Consider one crucial game near the end of the 1971–72 season. The year wasn't going well. Indiana, rated one of the league's top teams, was suffering frequent breakdowns on defense and disorganization on offense. All too often, the Pacers built up big leads over their opponents only to have things fall apart in the final quarter. They were struggling 5½ games behind Utah, the front-runners in the ABA Western Division. Indiana's fans were justifiably dissatisfied, but nothing could excuse their behavior in that particular late-season match.

The Pacers were playing Kentucky at home in a tight game. The crowd apparently felt the game was too tight; all the regulars were getting catcalls from the stands. Freddie Lewis, known to his teammates as "Fritz," spent most of the game sitting on the bench because Pacer coach Bob "Slick" Leonard had decided his team needed a shake-up. Second-year guard Rick Mount was started ahead of Fred. When it was clear the match would be won or lost in the final moments, Slick opted for experience in the backcourt and sent in Lewis.

Only a little over five minutes remained on the game clock when Freddie doffed his warm-up jacket and reported to the scorer's table prior to stepping on the court. Suddenly the Indianapolis Fairgrounds Coliseum erupted in a thunderous chorus of boos. It seemed as if every one of the 10,000 fans was jeering Freddie. Their cries grew even more deafening as Mount left the lineup and Lewis took his place. Many of the fans continued to boo Lewis even as the teams moved up and down the floor.

Indiana lost the game, 101–99, but that wasn't what upset the Pacer players. It was the crowd's unfair treatment of their veteran guard. All season long— and for some seasons before this—he had been the victim of the fans' wrath, but never had it been as blatant, as derisive as it was that night. In the locker room after the game, Lewis' teammates expressed their disgust in no uncertain terms.

"If our fans want to have a major league team,"

said forward Bob Netolicky, "then *they* have to learn to be major league. I think tonight's booing of Freddie was just a display of ignorance. Indiana's fans are great, but they've got to learn about people's feelings."

Said little Billy Keller: "They're treating Fritz so badly it's unbelievable. They're killing him! They say the fans pay for their seats and have the right to boo, but I don't think they're using good judgment to do that to a guy who's an Indiana Pacer."

By far the angriest reaction came from Mel Daniels, the Pacers' superstar center and Lewis' roommate on the road. "Those clowns are destroying my faith in people. How would they like it if we stood around and criticized them on their jobs? It's about time they showed some loyalty. What I'd like to know is why they are booing Freddie? What do you have to do to get accepted—do tricks? Do the fans have the right to destroy a man mentally?"

Continued the normally soft-spoken big man: "It was the first time I've ever come close to walking off the court when I heard them boo Freddie. It's to the point where you break your back to win and it doesn't mean anything. I guess we'll just have to consider every game a road game."

Lewis, meanwhile, quietly refused to answer questions, dressed quickly and left the locker room with a soft "See ya" in the direction of his fellow players. There was no ranting or raving on his part, only silent sadness.

Earlier in the season he had remarked: "Yes, I hear the boos and it hurts. As Slick says, I've sacrificed a lot to make myself an all-round ballplayer. I'm very sensitive. I like people and I like Indianapolis. It's my home now. There hasn't been a time when I refused a kid an autograph, and I've helped a lot of young people coming up. If I could just get the same kind of treatment from people as I give, I would be satisfied."

No one was ever able to explain why Freddie Lewis was the target of the boo-birds. Perhaps it was because he simply wasn't flashy enough for them. The Pacers have featured such outstanding big men as Daniels, Netolicky, Roger Brown and George McGinnis. They got most of the points and most of the attention from the press. Superstars may be forgiven a bad game or even a bad season, while the merely steady player becomes a scapegoat. It was Lewis who got the ball to the big guys and it was Lewis, a six-footer, who had to guard backcourtmen five and six inches taller than he. He hit the basket, too: Fritz averaged better than 20 points per game both of his first two years with Indiana.

"Everybody in Indianapolis gives Freddie a hard time," said Bob Leonard. "But let's face it—he's our captain; he calls our plays and sets up everybody. Freddie is our best guard. He does it all."

Lewis did everything except come from Indiana. The Pacers, along with every other ABA team, drafted college stars from their home state whenever possible. It made for instant fan recognition and

Indiana's Freddie Lewis is fouled from behind by San Antonio's Bob Warren.

boosted attendance. Interestingly, none of the Pacers' early heroes were local products. Mel Daniels played college ball at New Mexico, Brown at Dayton, Netolicky at Drake. Lewis, who was much more appreciated in his initial two years, was a graduate of Arizona State. Then the Pacers signed Billy Keller in 1969, and the seeds of conflict were sown.

A 5-foot-10 guard from Purdue, Keller was famous in Indiana even before he put on the blue and gold Pacer uniform. He had been a star at Washington High School in Indianapolis and later at Purdue, one of the state's two big-time universities. The fans expected to see him play, and the coach didn't disappoint them; Keller appeared in 82 of the 84 games in 1969–70, mostly as the backcourt partner of Freddie Lewis. But on those occasions when Fritz played and Keller didn't, the home crowd reacted negatively.

The situation worsened the following year when Rick Mount joined the team. Mount, who had played with Keller at Purdue, was a college superstar, a player who had received almost as much publicity as Pete Maravich, college basketball's most publicized player. Mount's greatest asset was his outside shooting, a real plus in a league that had a three-point shot from 25 feet out.

Mount could shoot, yes, but his ballhandling and defense were far below par. The fans' vision of a dream backcourt—Keller and Mount—was rudely shattered. Mount got some playing time—there were situations where his outside gunning came in handy. But he spent most of his time on the sidelines watching Lewis. The fans were restive and the owners (who had paid big money for Rick) were concerned.

Indiana had won the ABA title in 1969–70, but then lost to Utah in the semifinal in 1970–71, Mount's rookie year. The Pacers got off to a lumpy start in 1971–72, and the trend continued throughout the year even though they won more games than they lost. Slick Leonard experimented with various backcourt combinations including Mount and Keller. When Lewis played, he usually took Mount's place. When Fritz came off the bench and Rick came out of the game, the fans protested, even if Mount was doing a bad job. Lewis was booed often, and all the frustrations of what appeared to be a terrible season fell on Freddie's head.

Typically, Fritz down-played the fans' anger. "I think it's quite a natural reaction that they want to see their hometown boys play ahead of me," he insisted. "At times I feel badly, though, because they can't understand that I'm playing, scoring and helping out their ball club. I can't pinpoint why I am booed. I give a hundred percent of myself in each game."

Indiana stumbled into the 1972 playoffs with a 47–37 record. On the basis of their regular season performance, many experts predicted the team would be stopped in the first or second round. Those in the know, however, realized the Pacers were toughest

when the stakes were high, that they were a "money" team. And the man coach Leonard had dubbed his "money player" was not Daniels or Brown, but Freddie Lewis.

Fritz really lived up to his title. Indiana first faced a scrappy Denver team. The battle went seven games, and in the deciding match, played in Indianapolis, Lewis found himself splitting time with Mount. The Pacers were leading by nine at the end of the third quarter. Fritz had contributed ten points during one surge. Mount took over in the last quarter and the Rockets began battling back, narrowing Indiana's lead.

Freddie came off the bench again with 8:48 left in the contest. As usual, he was greeted with a refrain of loud jeers from the crowd. And as usual, he ignored the shouts and went about his work. His work was really cut out for him, too: guarding Denver's high-scoring guard, Ralph Simpson.

Simpson, who was 6-foot-5, couldn't get rid of his smaller opponent. He did everything possible to shake loose, but Lewis covered him like a bed sheet. Freddie was constantly in his way. Even on those rare instances when he got his hands on the ball, Simpson was so out of position he had no choice but to pass off or risk taking a bad shot.

On the other hand, Simpson had to guard Lewis, not an easy task. On one play Fritz took a pass from Daniels and cut past the big Rocket guard and several other Denver players for a cool lay-up. Even

Looking taller than his six-feet, Lewis grabs a rebound against Denver in the first round of the 1972 playoffs.

the hostile Coliseum fans had to cheer that play.

The two clubs fought down to the wire. Everything was at stake; the winner would face the Utah Stars in the next playoff round, while the losers would pack away their uniforms wondering what had gone wrong. The Rockets knew they couldn't win without the help of Simpson, and Lewis had held him scoreless for eight minutes.

Finally, with only 25 seconds to go and Denver down by two, Simpson was able to get free in one corner to pop a long jumper. The score was suddenly 89–all. The boo-birds were out in force now, calling Freddie every name in the book. Indiana quickly called a time-out, and as Leonard talked to his men, the fans screamed at him to put Mount back in for the last play.

It was clear that Indiana would hold on to the ball and run the clock down until they got a last, sure shot. All they had to do was keep the ball for a few moments, then get it in to one of their fine shooters, say Daniels or Roger Brown, for the winning shot.

There was no way Leonard was going to use Rick Mount then. What he wanted was reliable ballhandling and passing, and he looked to his team captain, Freddie Lewis. The Rockets, too, were very aware of the situation. As play resumed, Lewis dribbled about seeking an open big man. The Rockets decided to foul him, hoping he would miss one or both of the free throws and give Denver a few seconds to score again themselves.

The clock was stopped with less than ten seconds to play. Fritz went to the foul line with nary a peep from the crowd. The same people who had booed him during the game were now sitting anxiously on the edges of the seats with their fingers crossed. Lewis glanced at the clock, then took his first shot. Good! Then, his second. Good! Indiana was ahead by a slim margin, 91–89.

Denver got the ball, drove across the mid-court line and called a time-out. Four seconds—that's all that remained. Ten thousand fans were on their feet. Denver had one chance and one chance only: inbound the ball to a good shooter and have him shoot on the spot.

It was no surprise that the passer threw the ball in to Ralph Simpson. And it shouldn't have been any surprise that Freddie Lewis leaped high in the air to tip the ball out of bounds. Fritz' great defensive play wasted three seconds, seconds precious to Denver's cause.

The fate of the entire series now boiled down to one solitary second. Again the Rocket passer inbounded the ball toward Simpson. And again—incredibly—Lewis jumped in front of his man to deflect it away and end the game.

The next playoff round, against the Stars, was a duplicate of the Denver series right down to Freddie's seventh-game heroics. The last match with Utah saw Fritz give one of his finest performances of the year. Not only did he firmly guide the offense and play superb defense, he hit two foul shots with 24 seconds left to insure an Indiana victory. When the teams left the court, Freddie had scored 24 points, grabbed twelve rebounds and made six assists.

Lewis continued his torrid pace in the ABA championship series with the New York Nets. In the first game, which the Pacers won, 124–103, he scored 33 points (26 in the second half) and muzzled hot-shooting John Roche.

Freddie wasn't through yet. With the series tied at two games apiece, the fifth match wasn't going well for the Pacers. They trailed most of the contest, sometimes by as many as 20 points. But they pulled to within one point late in the game. With less than 20 seconds left, the Nets had possession and the game seemed over. Then Lewis stole the ball and was fouled as he drove for the hoop. You'd think the Nets would have learned from the Denver and Utah games: Fritz was the one Indiana player you shouldn't foul in the closing moments of a crucial game. Lewis had three chances to make two. His first shot rolled around the hoop and out. But his next two went in. Indiana won, 100–99, and went on to win their second ABA crown in the sixth game.

Fritz averaged 19.2 points and 4.4 assists in the 20 playoff games. He was named the Most Valuable Player of the post-season series.

"Freddie has been our most consistent player throughout the playoffs," said Bob Leonard. "He's

Lewis brings the ball downcourt during the championship series with New York.

played super ball. I can't understand why he doesn't get the respect of the fans at home. He certainly has the respect of the players who go against him."

"I always thought we had the talent to win it," said Fritz, "although we didn't have a particularly good season. It was my job to pass on that spirit to the other guys. I talked to them and tried to give them the confidence to win."

Confidence had never been a problem with Lewis. Freddie confidently left his hometown, McKeesport, Pennsylvania, for East Arizona Junior College and wound up with Little All-America honors after two years of play there. His next stop was Arizona State, where he averaged 25 points per game over two years. The NBA's Cincinnati Royals drafted him on the eighth round in 1966.

Fritz found himself on the bench behind pro basketball's greatest guard, Oscar Robertson, but he felt it was worth it: "Just being around Oscar has been a great help. He was great for me. He taught me the fundamentals of pro ball—how to move, how and when to shoot. He made me aware that there was room for the small guard in the pros, and showed me how to make use of size."

Freddie moved on to the newly formed ABA when it became apparent he wouldn't have much of a future with the Oscar-dominated Royals. Robertson had really had an effect, though. When Freddie joined the Pacers he chose the number 14—the same as that worn by the "Big O" in Cincinnati.

Lewis was an All-Star his first season with the Pacers, 1967–68. After that there was a dry spell. He played well, but there was a league rule for several years which allowed only three All-Star representatives from each team. The Pacers filled their berths with Daniels, Brown and Netolicky. When Netolicky was absent in 1972–73, Lewis again made the stellar squad.

If anyone needed proof of Freddie's fine play, they needed only to look in the ABA record book, where Fritz was well established among the top ten players in many categories. His name appeared most prominently in the all-time columns for regular season points (over 7,000), playoff free throws made (over 300), and regular-season and playoff assists.

Most telling, any doubter had to just look at the Pacers' record over the years. They were contenders every season since Freddy joined them, winning the title again in 1973 to become ABA champs for the third time in four years. Lewis was the backcourt leader every one of those years.

Although the fans seemed not to appreciate him, Freddie Lewis always had the last laugh.

8. GAIL GOODRICH

The Los Angeles Lakers had been playoff finalists for five straight years. But when the 1973–74 season got under way, they were in trouble. Their giant center, Wilt Chamberlain, had gone to coach in the ABA. And Jerry West, their great all-time All-Star, nearly retired, then was hobbled by injuries most of the year. Jim McMillian, their great young forward, was traded to Buffalo to obtain a replacement for Chamberlain. Who did coach Bill Sharman turn to and who became the new big name for the Lakers? Gail Goodrich.

Fate takes some strange turns, and the Lakers had once given up on the 6-foot-1 guard. Gail had to become a star on another team before he could become a star in his native Los Angeles. He had been drafted by the Lakers in 1965, only to spend most of his initial three years on the bench. Then he went to the newly formed Phoenix Suns and became their backcourt wizard. After two years, Phoenix traded him back to LA, making him the first man ever to go to an expansion club and be returned to his original team.

Gail was a born athlete if there ever was one. He was born with long arms and large hands—ideal for someone who would eventually be a guard. His father, Gail, Sr., had played basketball for the University of Southern California in the late 1930s. His mother lettered in basketball and several other sports in high school before going on to play for the Hollywood All-Stars, a famous women's touring softball team.

The Goodriches lived in the San Fernando Valley, a suburban section of Los Angeles. Gail's dad taught him the basics of basketball at an early age. They spent long hours together at local gyms and with their backyard equipment. Young Gail ate, drank and slept basketball. "When he was living at home," his mother recalled, "he was handling the ball all the time. He'd dribble the ball through the house so much that I thought he'd drive me out of my mind."

Gail had everything going for him except size. He was both short and skinny. Playing junior varsity ball in his tenth grade at Polytechnic High, he was just 5-foot-1, 99 pounds. He took his share of teasing from friends and teammates. Gail was good natured about the ribbing, but he once said to his parents: "I don't understand why God gave me all this ability and not the height to go with it."

Polytech won the city championship Gail's senior year. Now he was 6-foot-1—the tallest he would grow—and a skinny 135 pounds. Despite his frail appearance, Goodrich was one of the best guards in the LA school system, seemingly a prime college prospect.

Instead, colleges avoided him. No doubt many thought he was too small to play for them. Only two offered him athletic scholarships. The University of California at Los Angeles (UCLA) showed strong interest in him. And later, after Gail had decided on UCLA, crosstown rival Southern Cal—his father's college—showed some interest. Much as he would have liked following in his dad's footsteps, Gail was angry at USC for ignoring him until the last minute. He went to UCLA.

The excellent teaching of his father, coupled with good coaching from John Wooden, UCLA's famed mentor, ultimately paid off in Gail's junior year. He teamed in the backcourt with All-America and future NBA star Walt Hazzard, and the Bruins won 30 games, including a match with Duke for the national championship. Goodrich averaged 21 points a game.

As a senior he averaged 24.8 points and was named to several All-America teams. Again, the Bruins won the national title, this time whipping a strong Michigan team. Gail was the star of that game, throwing in 42 points. The match was carried on TV stations throughout the country, so people saw how a quick little man could undo much bigger opponents. The Lakers must have been watching, too. Soon after the match, Goodrich was chosen on the first round of the

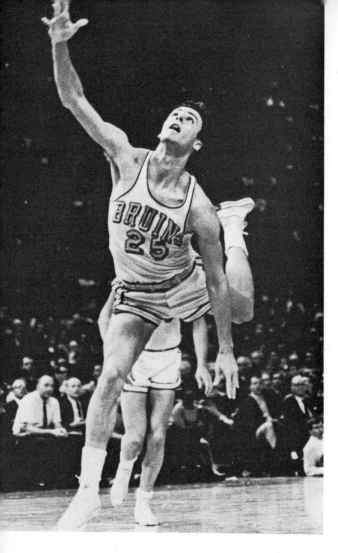

Off-balance, Gail puts in an amazing shot for UCLA during the 1965 NCAA finals.

NBA's very last territorial draft (pro teams then had exclusive rights over college players in their geographical area).

In 1965–66, Gail's rookie season, the number of 6-foot-1 players in the NBA could be counted on a single hand with fingers to spare. Earlier little men Slater Martin and Bob Cousy had retired. Nate

Archibald, Calvin Murphy and others were yet to come. Gail was a freak. Worse yet, he joined a veteran team with a backcourt starring a classic big guard, Jerry West.

Many observers thought that the only reason Goodrich was taken by the Lakers was his local fame. Few expected him to contribute significantly. Many of the LA regulars didn't take him seriously. His first day in training camp, All-Pro forward Elgin Baylor looked him over and labeled him "Stumpy" for his now-husky build. The name stuck even though his weight fluctuated during his early years with the team.

"When I first came into the league," Gail remembered, "everybody felt you had to be strong. That was the thing. They told me to put on weight. So I did. Then they said, 'You're too fat.' I couldn't please anyone."

Stumpy tried pleasing his coach, but that was a lost cause. Coach Fred Schaus had a reputation for not playing rookies. So Gail had to resign himself to making the most of his brief appearances and to absorbing as much as possible while on the sideline. There were long stretches when he never took off his warmup jacket. And when he did play, after sitting out a string of games, he was terrible.

In his second year he got a bit more playing time, averaging about 23 minutes a contest in 77 games. Still, his role was limited to giving the starters a breather. He played better, scoring 12 points per game, but no one seemed to notice.

Stumpy made an all-out effort in '67–68 to impress Bill Van Breda Kolff, the new coach who had replaced Schaus. He increased his scoring average to 13 points, yet he was nothing more than the team's number four guard. Gail was frustrated and angry. He figured he was better than fourth among the Laker backcourtmen. A future on the Los Angeles bench was no future at all, as far as Goodrich was concerned. It was time to move on.

It so happened that the NBA was expanding for the 1968–69 season. Four new franchises were being added to the league, representing San Diego, Milwaukee, Phoenix and Seattle. Each established club was allowed to protect six players on its roster, and the rest could be drafted by the new teams. Gail saw his chance. At the end of the '67–68 season he asked to go to an expansion team. Although there was no indication the Laker management was going to protect him, he wasn't taking any chances. "I was happy to leave Los Angeles," he noted candidly. "I didn't care where I went, just so I left the Lakers."

Phoenix grabbed him at the first opportunity. "Every team needs a leader," announced Suns coach Johnny Kerr just after picking Goodrich, "and Gail has filled this spot both in college at UCLA and with the Lakers. He's an experienced player who's accustomed to winning, and we're looking to him to provide spark and leadership."

Kerr got exactly what he wanted. Stumpy established himself as Phoenix's backcourt mainstay from

As a Laker rookie, Gail looks smaller than ever against the towering form of the Celtics' big man, Bill Russell (6).

the start of the '68–69 season. He had a lot of adjustments to make. Suddenly, he was playing 40 minutes of every match. Suddenly, everyone was looking for him to make the big plays against defenses that were waiting for him.

He was a fine outside shooter, but he also liked to get inside. "In college ball," he remarked, "there are five opposing players and ten hands. In pro ball, there are five players and 20 hands. But that doesn't stop me from driving. I've adjusted my inside shots and passes and am never afraid to traipse down the middle."

Traipsing down the middle had its disadvantages, like some big guy planting an elbow in his face. Stumpy, however, refused to be intimidated into giving up his inside game. "Lack of height never discouraged me," he stated during his first year at Phoenix, "and I don't feel it is a great handicap now, even in the NBA. I could use some weight, though. At 175, I get banged around a lot."

And Goodrich banged the opposition around with his shooting and playmaking. In fact, he led the Suns in both departments in '68–69. His scoring (23.8 points per game) was third best among the NBA's guards. He was Phoenix's captain and an All-Star.

He was great on defense, too. "Gail gives me fits on defense," said teammate Dick Snyder, a 6-foot-5 guard. "I don't relish working against him in practice because he's so quick, but it does me good and I learn a lot from him."

Despite several 40-plus-point nights (including 43 against the Lakers), Stumpy couldn't pull his team out of the lower depths of the Western Division standings. Phoenix finished near the bottom its first year. The next season, 1969–70, the Suns managed to secure a playoff spot (although they were eliminated in the first round), and Gail was wonderful. Again, he was high in scoring (20 points a game) and assists (seven a game, fifth best in the NBA).

Gail set an example by playing well in the face of adversity. In February 1970, he suffered a bruised heel one practice session. The injury was extremely painful, and over a four-game period his scoring dropped to less than ten points a game. All four matches were lost, throwing Phoenix into a divisional tie with Seattle. Then came a game with those same SuperSonics. With a possible playoff spot at stake, both teams were fired up.

Goodrich, his bad foot tightly bandaged, played what was perhaps his finest game as a Sun that night. He had an immediate challenge in guarding Seattle's player-coach (and renowned little man), Lenny Wilkens. Phoenix's young coach, Jerry Colangelo, explained the matchup by saying, "I thought it would help bring out the best in Gail."

It did. Wilkens fell into early foul trouble trying to stop Goodrich on defense and trying to get past him on offense. Bruised heel or no, Stumpy scored 16 points in the first quarter, sending Lenny to the bench in disgust. Wilkens played only 17 minutes of the game. None of the men who took his place opposite Goodrich could handle the Phoenix flash. Gail was all over the court popping incredible shots, zipping passes to teammates when the Sonics double-teamed him, and playing impenetrable defense.

Phoenix won, 129–118. Gail finished with 44 points, making 17 of 26 shots from the field and 10 of 11 from the foul line. He also had ten assists.

By rights, Goodrich should have had a long, comfortable stay in Phoenix. His career was progressing, he loved the city, its fans and the climate. The only thing missing, in his opinion, was enough money. The Suns' superstar forward, Connie Hawkins, was being paid a small fortune in salary. Gail figured he was just as valuable to the team as the Hawk, and should be paid accordingly. The owners didn't see it his way, so Stumpy asked to be traded.

One story is that as Gail and his wife left for a European vacation at the close of the '69–70 season, Jerry Colangelo (who was also Phoenix's general manager) asked him: "Where shall I send your bags?"

Goodrich wasn't partial, but he got a shock when those bags wound up in Los Angeles. Yes, the Suns had traded him back to the Lakers. Phoenix exchanged Gail for LA's reserve center, Mel Counts.

Laker coach Joe Mullaney was elated by the Goodrich trade. "He's the kind of guard we need," said Mullaney prior to the start of the 1970–71 campaign. "He moves the ball well. He can get it up the floor under pressure and he penetrates very well. He's a proven shooter also, which should eliminate some of the double-teaming tactics used against West last season."

Stumpy wasn't quite as enthusiastic. "I have to view this trade with some mixed emotions. I wasn't happy my first three years with the Lakers because I didn't get to play much. Then in Phoenix I played a lot and my wife and I got to love that town. Of course, Los Angeles is our home and I have some very good friends on the Lakers in Jerry West and Elgin Baylor. I also think I'm a much better player than I was two years ago, so that should change the situation."

Gail was a starter, just as he had been at Phoenix, but playing with the Lakers was an entirely new experience. To begin with, LA was a higher-scoring, better-balanced squad. West and newcomer Jim McMillian were super shooters. Where the Suns had lacked a strong center, LA had Wilt Chamberlain, one of the best in the history of the game. Jerry West was also the team's playmaker.

Stumpy averaged 17.5 points for the 1970–71 regular season. He hadn't played his best. He had put on some extra pounds in Europe, and he looked sluggish much of the time. And he had to adjust to being without the ball, letting West set the offense and make the assists.

Only during the '71 playoffs did he show what he could do. The Lakers had had major injuries throughout '70–71, the worst being a torn knee ligament sustained by West just before the playoffs. Gail took over as backcourt leader while Jerry watched from the sidelines—a portent of things to come. The wounded Lakers barely beat Chicago, then were demolished by a Milwaukee club that would go on to win the 1971 NBA title. Goodrich had averaged 25.4 points and had 91 assists in the 12 games, his finest playoff statistics.

Neither Goodrich nor the Laker management wanted a repeat of '70–71. Los Angeles made a positive step in hiring Bill Sharman as the team's new coach. Sharman, a former NBA All-Star forward, arrived fresh from coaching the Utah Stars to an ABA championship.

Stumpy was determined to make the most of his strengths, beginning with an exhaustive program of conditioning in the off-season. Working under UCLA track coach Jim Bush, he ran his heart out. He started slowly, gradually increasing his distances and times. Before he was through, he could run four miles without pause. Bush added more exotic forms of training. "Running up and down the bleachers wasn't enough for coach Bush," said Gail. "He even had me *hopping* up the bleachers."

As a result, he went to the '71–72 training camp in the best shape of his pro career. His legs were powerful, his wind was much improved and his endurance was fantastic. Luckily so, because Sharman carried Bush's philosophy onto the court—run,

run, run. The coach was pleased with Gail's condition, for he wished to enlarge Stumpy's role. Sharman felt the little man's talents had been wasted the season before, and that Gail was more than just a guy who happened to be playing in the same backcourt with Jerry West. He wanted Gail to shoot more and handle the ball more, so he installed a wide-open, running offense.

Things clicked for the Lakers in 1971–72. During the season they set a pro basketball record with an amazing 33-game win streak and had the best won-lost record in NBA history. Gail was instrumental in both achievements.

In December 1971, the Lakers were playing Phoenix at Los Angeles. If they won, they would tie the NBA record of 20 straight victories set by Milwaukee the year before. The Suns, who had won eight in a row, were hungry to stop them. They almost did, forcing the game into overtime.

That's when Gail really turned it on, destroying his old team's chances with brilliant jump shots. He launched two key shots, from 20 and 15 feet, that took the fire out of the Suns. Then, with 1:42 left in the extra session, he pounced on a loose ball, dribbled through a forest of Phoenix men to the top of the foul circle and tossed in a shot to put the match out of reach. The Lakers won, 126–117. Stumpy led all scorers with 32 points.

"I thought we had the momentum going our way in the overtime," said a sad Cotton Fitzsimmons, the

Suns' coach, following the match, "but a guy named Goodrich thought otherwise. If he'd been playing in the other league with that three-pointer, he'd have had about 45 points tonight."

After the regular season, the Lakers went on to win their first NBA championship. In their ten years in Los Angeles they had qualified for the championship every year, but until 1972, they had never won.

The 1971–72 campaign was a milestone in Stumpy's career. Not only did he play on his first championship team, but he led that team in regular-season scoring with a 25.9-point average. Significantly, he was a starter for the West squad in the '72 All-Star Game, easing out perennial favorite Oscar Robertson. He would again start in the 1974 All-Star Game.

Gail kept up his point-making the next year, even though the Lakers lost to New York in the championship round. He averaged 23.9 ppg in the 1972–73 regular season and 20 ppg in the playoffs.

Jerry West was out with injuries for most of the 1973–74 season, prompting speculation that it would be his last year in a long, illustrious career. Naturally, people wanted to know if Gail felt he could replace West in the hearts and minds of the Los Angeles fans and in the NBA record book. "I don't think Jerry can be replaced," Gail answered truthfully.

Stumpy wasn't out to replace West or anyone else. He just played the game his way. By any standards— big or small—Gail Goodrich was good enough.

Attempting a lay-up, Goodrich has the ball swatted out of his hands by Detroit's big center, Bob Lanier.

9. DEAN MEMINGER

Dean Meminger was a hard man to beat, as Calvin Murphy discovered one afternoon in 1973. Meminger, a 6-foot-1 defensive specialist with the Knicks, faced the 5-foot-9 Murphy in a game between New York and Houston. In a relatively dull game, the battling little guards provided the sparks. The partisan Houston crowd was really jolted in the second quarter.

A Knick took a shot that bounced high off the rim. Murphy, whose leaping ability was legendary, soared into the air to snag the rebound. Before anyone could blink, he was headed in the opposite direction with Meminger in desperate pursuit. Murphy was probably the fastest man on the dribble in the league, and he had more than a step on Dean at the midcourt line. There was no one between him and the basket.

Calvin never got there. About 20 feet from the basket, Meminger—running at his top speed—leaned forward, stretched out one of his long arms and

flicked the ball away from Murphy right into the hands of Knick forward Phil Jackson. As the Rockets converged on Jackson, he threw the ball back to Dean, who sped in for an uncontested score.

Meminger came to the Knicks in 1971. In his first seasons he wasn't known for his scoring or playmaking—given enough playing time, he was good for ten points and a couple of assists a game. No, what New York expected of him was defense. And Dean played defense better than any little man in pro basketball, with the possible exception of Norm Van Lier.

Oddly, Dean had been a super-scorer in high school and college. He was regarded as one of the finest young shooters ever to leave New York City. He made All-America at Marquette University mainly because of his ability to put the ball in the net, and it was an important factor in his being a number one draft pick of the Knicks.

Dean was born in Walterboro, South Carolina, a small community about 40 miles from Charleston. He grew up in a strong, close-knit family. His parents stressed values and the need for an education. "I had a built-in value system," Meminger remembered. "A lot of kids have none. I knew when I was young, I had some goals. When I was nine, I played organized basketball in grammar school. When I was 12 or 13, I was averaging 42 points a game. I had a mother to confide in. I had to stay in school. I played ball and then came home to do my homework. There was no time to hang around the streets."

The Memingers moved to New York City's Harlem when Dean was 13. The lure of the streets was much stronger in Harlem than it was in Walterboro. New York was a whole other scene—there he was exposed to drugs, crime, despair. But Dean survived the crippling environment because he had loving parents to turn to in times of distress, and because he had basketball. He did so well in junior high and on the schoolyard courts that several high school coaches tried to recruit him for their teams. Meminger narrowed his choice down to Power Memorial and Rice, rival Catholic high schools with mighty basketball reputations. He chose Rice in the end because Power's star was Lew Alcindor (now Kareem Abdul-Jabbar), and Dean didn't fancy playing in the shadow of the best schoolboy hoopster in the city.

Alcindor, who was two years ahead of Dean, soon became the first New Yorker ever named All-City three times. Meminger was the second. From the tenth grade on, the stands at every Rice game were filled with college scouts evaluating Dean. By the end of his senior season, every major basketball power— and a shipload of minor ones—was trying to get him to sign up. He could have gone to any one of hundreds of universities on full athletic scholarship, yet only two really attracted him—UCLA and Marquette.

Marquette was a Catholic school (Dean's faith), it had a growing basketball program coached by a New Yorker and—this was the clincher—it didn't have

Lew Alcindor on its squad. The giant center was already an All-America at UCLA, and again Meminger couldn't see himself following in the big guy's wake. Meminger went to Marquette.

Under coach Al McGuire, Dean led the Warriors to 78 wins in 87 regular- and post-season games. Marquette's stature among the great college teams grew. Meminger was the very first Marquette player to gain All-America honors. He scored 1,637 points over three varsity years and made better than 50 percent of his field goals. He averaged 21 points per game as a senior, and guided his team to a 28–1 record.

Dean made perhaps his best showing as a junior in the 1970 National Invitational Tournament (NIT) at New York's Madison Square Garden. Marquette turned down a bid to play in the more prestigious NCAA tournament for the NIT. Besides wanting his team to play for the crowds and the cameras in New York, coach Al McGuire wanted to match Meminger against such glittering hot-shots as Pete Maravich (Louisiana State), Charlie Scott (North Carolina) and Julius Erving (Massachusetts).

Marquette was favored to win the tourney, and that's exactly what they did. First Massachusetts fell to them, then Utah, after a 28-point performance from Dean. Next, Marquette crushed Maravich and LSU, 101–79. In the championship game, Marquette rolled over St. John's, 65–53.

A determined Dean Meminger gets off a shot for Marquette during the 1970 NIT, while his St. John's defender bends over backwards to avoid fouling him.

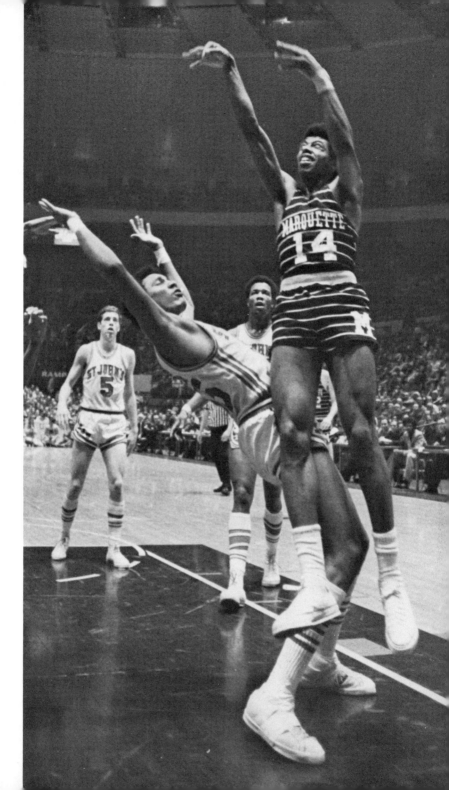

Perhaps guys like Maravich, Scott and Erving had come into the tournament with more press clippings, but it was Dean Meminger who walked away with the Most Valuable Player trophy. He had scored a total of 71 points in four games while quarterbacking the Warrior attack and playing sturdy defense. Local fans may have been disappointed that St. John's—a New York school—lost, but at least it was to a club led by a New York coach and a New York star.

The MVP award meant more than just national publicity to Dean. It meant he had come a long way from the concrete courts of his youth. "I've been playing basketball for 14 years," he said after accepting the trophy. "There was nothing much else you could do when you were growing up in a disadvantaged area like I did.

"When we were kids and interested in an education, the first thing we picked up around the schoolyards and playgrounds is that if you learn to play basketball real well, it's a passbook to a college education. So you play and play hard, every day. When I was in grammar school, hardly a day went by that we didn't play two or three hours. Then, when I was attending Rice High School, I would sometimes play two and three games a day."

He continued, "Someone asked me how I felt about playing against Pete Maravich the other day. I don't want to take anything away from Pistol Pete, but we had better players competing in the schoolyards and playgrounds who never got to college."

Al McGuire had given Meminger the nickname "Dean the Dream" because the little man was a coach's dream. Al's brother, Dick, more than agreed with the title. Dick was then the New York Knicks' chief scout, so naturally everyone wanted to know his evaluation of the Marquette marvel.

"If I were to hand in a scouting report on Dean right now," Dick stated, "it would go something like this: 'Reminds me of Lenny Wilkens [then the player-coach of the Seattle SuperSonics] when he played at Providence. Quick hands, penetrates real well, excellent ballhandler, good jumper. Don't know how well he can shoot from the outside.' "

That's just about the scouting report he did turn in one year later, at the close of Marquette's 1970–71 season. The Knicks picked Dean on the first round of the college draft largely on the strength of Dick McGuire's recommendation. When asked about Meminger's outside shooting, McGuire answered jokingly, "Dean has a great outside shot, although you'd never know it watching him play at Marquette where Al thought he was a pivotman or something, the way he used him."

Meminger never actually played center for the Warriors. He did, however, often wind up under the hoop on offense. Marquette used a set-play offense. Dean not only brought the ball down and called the plays, he also drove inside and often scored from close in. He wasn't one to pop from the outside.

Dick went on to state: "He's good at the kind of

aggressive defense we try to play, and I don't think his size will be too much against him." Size, as it turned out, was a factor in Dean's favor.

Before Meminger, the Knicks always went for tall guards in their drafts. In the two years prior to 1971, they had taken John Warren of St. John's and Mike Price of Illinois. Warren and Price wound up warming the New York bench. Price was eventually cut, and Warren was left unprotected in the 1970 expansion draft and taken by one of the new teams. If these big young guards couldn't make it with the team, why did New York pick a little fellow like Meminger?

Defense, that's why. And particularly defense against men such as Calvin Murphy and Nate Archibald. Knicks owner Ned Irish explained it this way: "A lot of small, quick guards are coming into the league and we've had trouble handling some of them. We've rounded out our squad by getting someone under 6-2."

Dean proved much more than his defensive worth one night early in his rookie year against the Los Angeles Lakers. Acting as a substitute in place of Dick Barnett, Meminger found himself facing veteran Gail Goodrich.

He came off the bench in the third quarter to open the Knicks' 67–60 lead. Dave DeBusschere attempted to pass to fellow Knick Jerry Lucas, only to have the ball deflected. Meminger alertly scooped up the loose ball and scored. Then there was a play in which the 24-second clock was winding down dangerously. Meminger got the ball and calmly worked himself

Playing great defense for the Knicks in 1973, Meminger makes things tough for another small guard, Cleveland's Lenny Wilkens.

open for a good shot while his teammates on the bench screamed, "Red! Red!"—the signal that he had to shoot quickly or risk a penalty for violating the clock. Dean took his time, refusing to be ruffled. He made his shot without a second to spare.

He also brought the Garden fans to their feet with his daring rebounding. Once he and Knick center

Willis Reed (6-foot-9) went up together for a rebound. Meminger came down with the ball. Meminger would soon be recognized as the best rebounder for his size in all of pro basketball.

That night, Dean finished with 15 points, six assists and seven rebounds—fine statistics for a non-starter. More important, he held Goodrich to just 14 points—a major reason for New York's 126–114 victory. And he had shown a marked ability to control the New York offense when he had to. "It's the first time," said Laker assistant coach K. C. Jones, "that I've ever seen a rookie come in and handle the ball that much. He's a smart player. The way New York plays team ball, he fits in beautifully."

Los Angeles' great guard, Jerry West, also had glowing praise for Meminger. "The impressive thing about him is he's got a lot of poise. He doesn't seem to get excited."

Meminger's rookie year wasn't spectacular from a statistical standpoint. He averaged four points and an assist per game. However, he did get in 15 minutes a game playing time. That meant a bad-kneed guard like Earl Monroe could get 15 minutes rest and, from the team's viewpoint, a well-rested Monroe was essential. It was also important, of course, that Monroe's replacement carry his own weight, and Meminger did.

The 1971–72 Knicks made it to the championship playoffs only to be defeated by the Lakers. Dean's most important playoff contribution came in the semifinals with Boston. The Knick backcourt starters, Monroe and Walt Frazier, got into early foul trouble in the second game between the clubs. New York coach Red Holzman threw Dean into the fray. Meminger took immediate charge, handling the ball, feeding teammates, and going inside himself for 12 points in spite of the big guys.

Dean also did a creditable defensive job on the Celtics' 6-foot-3 JoJo White. "Defense is consistent, offense is fickle," he explained after the game. "I feel everyone does something better than anything else and it's my job to know what it is. When White brings the ball up, I try to break him down, make him work ten or eleven seconds, so he wants to give it up. That limits the Celtics in what they can do."

There seemed no limit to what Dean could do that night. He blocked three Boston shots, all from men several inches taller than he. He got a couple of steals. He went to the boards for six rebounds. And to top things off, he frustrated a Celtic inbounds play with a minute and a half left in the game, forcing them to take a time out and come back with a hurry-up shot that missed, giving New York a 106–105 win.

The next season, 1972–73, was a replay of the last, except that the Knicks beat Los Angeles for the NBA crown. Meminger's playing time and scoring increased slightly (18 minutes and 5 points a game). He didn't let his substitute status bother him. "It's a long season," he stated, "and you get a chance to play along the way." On another occasion, he said, "My main objective is to perfect my abilities within this New York system. The Knicks are a team-oriented club which allows a person to develop and work within the system."

Unlike most little men, Dean didn't have a good outside shot. And unlike most small guys, he willingly traded muscle with tough forwards and centers. He often grabbed an offensive rebound and went straight for the hoop, schoolyard style.

"I'm quicker and faster than the average guard in the NBA," he explained, "and that's a big asset. But a lot of what I do on the court has to do with growing up in New York and the style of ball we played here. In the playground you learned that the guy who got the rebound got to shoot the ball. It was a matter of survival. Nobody was going to fight for a rebound and give up the ball.

"Playground ball is no place for specialization. Versatility is what counts. You have to learn to shoot, dribble and rebound. There is also no time for being afraid of getting hurt. You play against them all, big and small, and battle them all."

Once again, Meminger shone in the 1973 playoffs. And once again, Boston was the victim. In the seventh and deciding match of the semifinals, Dean helped put the Knicks over the top with another brilliant defensive effort on JoJo White, 13 points of his own (nine in a second quarter rally), and six rebounds. Said a happy coach Holzman: "On defense, Dean was just great. But, then, he's capable of

A giant leap puts Dean way up there for the rebound with teammate Dave DeBusschere in the 1973 playoffs against Boston.

that type of game. I never thought of taking him out after the first half. He was making the team do things."

Dean devoted his summers to coaching and counseling ghetto kids. He understood the problems of these youngsters, having experienced them himself.

"The kids look around and who do they have to emulate?" he asked. "Who is there to inspire and stimulate them? Athletes, entertainers, pimps and hustlers. They see Cadillacs and figure it takes $25,000 a year. If a kid hasn't got the skills, he becomes a hustler. Even if he gets an education, he is lowest on the job market. If he can get a quick dollar, that's all that counts. Sometimes I come home and I'm pessimistic. Instead of getting better, it's getting worse. But I can't give up. We're the last hope for these kids."

Meminger entered the 1973–74 season with a new role—starter—because of an injury to Earl Monroe. Earl returned at midseason and finished strongly, however, and in May 1974 the Knicks left Meminger unprotected in the expansion draft for the new NBA team in New Orleans.

Dean was the first player picked by New Orleans. Then he went straight to the Atlanta Hawks as part of a trade for superstar Pete Maravich. Meminger was sorry to leave the Knicks and New York, but he was also flattered to be picked first in the draft and he looked forward to being a starter and a big contributor to the Hawks.

INDEX

Page numbers in italics refer to photographs.